A *Favor*

Presented to

_____

Given by

_____

_____

Date

WHAT OTHERS SAY...

"DO YOURSELF A FAVOR" is a must read! Feel burned out, depressed, bored with life? Read this book and see how the "Master" Jesus Christ can lead you into a new and better life filled with peace and wisdom."
Joe Black, author of "Attitude Connection", "Looking Back on the Future" and "Passing Through".

". . . In a world so desperate for encouragement and hope this book is an answer to prayers. It is a light to a dark world - God's love shows through the author's pen, so Do Yourself A Favor.
Greg Finley - Founder - Right Road Ministry, Inc.
Publisher of Right Road Magazine

"The gentle advice to be found in Frieda Baird's book is, on the face of it, simple and straight forward. Careful consideration of her anecdotes, however, reveals a Christian wisdom that emerges from deep personal experience. It is this experience that both validates her advice and charges it with authority and compassion. This is a book I will keep close at hand; one I will return to often."
David Crossman, author - *"Murder in a Minor Key" (Carroll & Graf, New York, NY - 1994)*
"You Can't Get Where You're Not Going" (Penobscot Books, Rockland, ME - 1996)
"A Show of Hands" (Down East Books, Camden, ME - 1997)
"Bean and Ab: The Masterpiece Mystery" (Down East Books, Camden, ME 1998)
"The Dead of Winter" (Down East Books, Camden, ME - 1999)
Christian song writer and recording atist -
"Footprints On My Wings" (Out of the Whirlwind Records, 1991)
"Whose Fool Are You?" (Out of the Whirlwind Records, 1995)
"Which Way to the Coliseum?" (Out of the Whirlwind Records, 1996)
"Filet of Soul" (Out of the Whirlwind Records, 1998)

Your Life is About to Change...

DO YOURSELF A FAVOR

Finally, Overcome Fears, Hurts And Failures.

Gain New Insights To Encourage And Appreciate Yourself.

FROM THE SERIES

LET US REMEMBER

VOLUME ONE

By

FRIEDA YOUNG BAIRD

NEW VENTURE
P.O. BOX 26493
GREENVILLE, SC 29616

Published by
NEW VENTURE
P.O. Box 26493, Greenville, SC 29616

This book is written to provide encouragement. It is sold with the understanding that the publisher and author are not engaged in rendering counseling or other professional services. If counseling or other expert assistance is required, the services of a competent professional should be sought.

The purpose of this book is to relate the author's experiences and teachings. The author and publisher shall have neither liability nor responsibility to any person or entity with respect to any loss or damage caused, or alleged to be caused, directly or indirectly by the information contained in this book. If you do not wish to adhere to the previous statements, you may return this book to the publisher for a refund of the purchased price.

ISBN 0-9664044-1-6
Library of Congress Catalog Card Number: 98-91551

Cover design and illustrations by Jim Baird.

PRINTED IN THE UNITED STATES OF AMERICA

"THANK YOU"...

I owe this book first and foremost to the faithfulness and enabling of our Lord and Savior Jesus Christ. He has used His earthly vessels to encourage and direct me from its inception. My artist husband began with, *"Why don't you put all these notes that are spread all over the house into a book?"* My family, Dawne, Victor, Emily, Barbara and Lib responded during the writing with, *"I'm proud of you, Mom." "How's the book coming Frieda?" "You can do it!"*

Jim, you understand more than any other the trials and frustrations that have occurred during its writing. You always were there to pull me up to start again. Without your help and talents, the book would still be in note form. I'll always love you for it. Family, you 'hung' in there with me helping with your comments and skills. Mega *"thank you"* with much love.

God's vessels have been assorted. Many were used directly such as Tonya and David Hodel along with Stacey Jillson who did the editing and became friends for life. Rich and Karen Bigger, Susie Harvey, David Crossman, Mike and Diana Schaff and Joe Black were all instruments who had a special role in development of this work. Often you did not know how much I needed your help and encouragement and hung on your every word for my next step.

David Crossman, my talented and treasured brother in the Lord, *"thank you"* for the helpful editing and suggestions that were needed and so appreciated. Mike and Diana you placed more steps for me to climb and helped me climb them. Joe, your encouraging books and caring words helped me on my journey.

A special *"thanks"* to my dear, patient, giving friend Darrell Duncan for his sacrificial hours of helping me learn the strange and foreboding world of computer software. *"Thank you"* George and Barbara Corell, owners of Millie Lewis Modeling Agency, for your enthusiasm, assistance and talents.

Also, the Merritt 'clan' Tom, Jeanine, Wayne and Mary for listening and helping. *"Thank you,"* Jeanine, for the final proofing. Is everything spelled OK? I also appreciate and cherish the love and God's blessing to me in Trish and David Richardson who with Wes and Betty McMillan kept me together with their loving prayer support. How I needed it! Also *"thank you"*, my long time and lifetime friends, Don and Evelyn Reynolds who once again graciously opened their home where one of the unknown 'steps' became known.

The acknowledgements for a book are more complex than we realize because books are the results of interactions and actions. People make up our lives and experiences. They become our partners in our steps of life. ***"Thank you all for making this book possible."***

INTRODUCTION

Have you ever said *"Blechhh!"* when you looked at yourself in the mirror? I have, and the still small voice of the Lord spoke to me one morning saying, *"Why don't you do yourself a favor and accept yourself?"* He lovingly showed me the reason my inferiority developed and how to love and accept myself. You will find my story of deliverance in the following pages under the title, "DO YOURSELF A FAVOR."

At the death of a family friend, I was reminded of a saying my mother used to tell me, *"Don't send me any flowers after I'm gone!"* In other words, any kind words or actions you have for me, show me now while I can enjoy them. Don't wait until I'm gone and speak them at my funeral. I sadly realized I had not sent our friend any 'verbal' flowers while he was alive. My life had become too busy for this needful expression of appreciation.

I also remembered my only brother who was tragically killed in an automobile accident. At his death, my grief was beyond words. We argued the night before his accident and my final words to him were angry and bitter. Freed from this persistent torment, I was able to write about my victory under the title, "DON'T SEND ME ANY FLOWERS."

Many of us have messy closets in our lives. I'm not referring to the place we hang our clothes, but our emotional closets. The Lord tenderly healed me of the pain and suffering I experienced as a child - pain caused by violent, alcoholic parents. He marvelously cleaned and straightened my emotional messy closets with a stroke of His compassionate hand. I relived this healing as I wrote the story entitled, "MESSY CLOSETS."

Have you ever had a tyrant for an employer? My husband has, and we experienced the intense frustration of delay in answered prayers concerning a man with an explosive temper. However, the Lord revealed to us "IN DUE SEASON" that we will reap the fruit of answered prayer if we continue to believe His promises. We did and experienced the victory of His miracle!

During the writing of this book I had to "DRAW THE LINE" on numerous attempts by the enemy to defeat me. I have "LOOKED TOO LONG" at the obstacles in my life and started to sink. My resolve to "WALK IN LOVE" was tested often and I forced myself to renew my mind and exercise my "MENTAL MUSCLES" daily. These are samples of real life trials and hardships with a common theme. Each story is an encouragement to us that shows the Lord's desire and enabling for our victories.

My good friend, author, David Crossman, recently wrote of the value of sharing our life experiences. His words were so poetic I will not try to enlarge upon them. They are words to all of us. He wrote, *"I think it is so important for people with a rich Christian experience to share the things the Lord has taught them through the triumphs and tragedies of life so that others will know that, despite the unfamiliarity of the path, it has been traveled before and they don't travel alone."*

This has been a journey for me and I pray it will be for you. We all have one overriding purpose, to draw closer to our Lord in all that we do. Let me encourage you to not give up during the journey. Different emotions and distractions divert us from His purpose, but as we encourage one another, we can press on and run the race with endurance. Life is a wonderful gift from our Father. Each chapter in this book will help you "do yourself a favor"and enjoy your life to the fullest every day!

May the Lord bless you and "LET US REMEMBER" that He loves us tremendously and desires for us to be all that we can be. Receive these encouragements with my love.

ABOUT THE AUTHOR

Born into a poor, violent, alcoholic family in 1945, Frieda Young Baird worked very hard throughout her school years and young adult life to overcome the stigma of her parents' dysfunctions.

Frieda frequently draws from her personal, inner well of God granted healing and victories from the violence, shame, and tragedies of her life as well as the pain resulting from the deaths of her parents and her older brother. These insights and personal healing coupled with her deep relationship with Jesus have given her a unique talent to encourage and build up others. Throughout the years, Frieda has written her thoughts and discoveries with the hope of fulfilling a desire to reach others with the healing power of Christ's love.

ABOUT THE ARTIST

Jim Baird was born in 1944 in a small town in the coal mining district of Kentucky. He attended and graduated in 1964 with a Associates of Arts degree from Southern Illinois University.

Since graduating, Jim has gained over 34 years of experience as an illustrator and graphic designer. During this time, he supervised and personally handled the design, illustration and production of printed advertising for national and regional accounts. He is also currently pursuing his love of portraiture rendering.

X

CONTENTS

THANK YOU V

INTRODUCTION VII

ABOUT THE AUTHOR - ARTIST X

A LOYAL FRIEND 13

BELIEVE FOR YOUR DREAM 17

CHOCOLATE-COVERED CHERRIES 21

CORRUPT COMMUNICATIONS 25

"DO YOURSELF A FAVOR" 29

DON'T LOOK TOO LONG! 33

"DON'T SEND ME ANY FLOWERS" 37

DRAW THE LINE 41

EMPTY YOUR POCKETS! 45

FOUR MORE YARDS! 49

GOING HOME 51

HEAR THE HIS-S-S 57

"I HATE DIETS" 61

"I NEED MY LOVIN'!" 65

"I NEVER GOT TO SAY GOODBYE!" 69

"I'M DANCING AS HARD AS I CAN !" 73

IN DUE SEASON 77

"IS MY ARM TOO SHORT?. 83

LOAD OUR GUNS 87

MENTAL MUSCLES .93

MESSY CLOSETS 97

"MY CHILD DON'T EVER
STOP LOVING ME" 103

NOT HOW, BUT WHO 107

OUR RESPONSIBILITY IS TO RECEIVE 111

RING AND SANDALS 115

SYMPTOMS 119

THE SPIRIT OF XMAS 123

THE WALLS CAME TUMBLING DOWN 125

WALK IN LOVE 131

WINGS 135

"YOU'LL HAVE TO SPEAK UP,
SHE'S HARD OF HEARING" 139

CLOSING. 141

A LOYAL FRIEND

"And the scripture was fulfilled that says, 'Abraham believed God, and it was credited to him as righteousness,' and he was called God's friend." (James 2:23) (NIV)

Those of us who have children know the ache in our hearts when with pools of sadness in their tender eyes and faces wet with overflowing tears they whisper softly, *"No one likes me. I don't have a friend."*

Have you ever wanted "a loyal friend?" Perhaps you have the good fortune of already having one. The need to have someone with whom to share our thoughts, dreams and laughter begins in our childhoods. As we grow older, our need for this type of relationship intensifies; however, sometimes we protect our vulnerability by saying, *"That's childish." "I can be strong by myself." "Who needs it?"*

It is important to have "a loyal friend", but it is also important *to be* "a loyal friend"- one who consistently shows faithfulness. Though wrong and hurtful things are said about you by other people, a loyal friend will support and stand up for you without having to have proof of your innocence.

Remember when your loyal friend stood up for you and took your side? It made you feel stronger and not so alone. Faithful and loyal friendship is a prized possession indeed.

With this consideration in mind, we can examine loyalty in friendship in more than one way. Proverbs 18:24 tells us, ". . . there is a friend who sticks closer than a brother." (NIV) We all have a friend who sticks closer than a brother and this friend has shown Himself to have the utmost loyalty. His name is Jesus.

When things go wrong in our lives, often the first one we blame is God. When a prayer is not answered as we hoped, we may accuse Him of lack of love or concern. Even the disciples, fearing their lives were in danger, questioned His concern for them. In Mark 4:38,40 when the waves of the sea were filling the boat, they exclaimed, *"Teacher, don't you even care that we are all about to drown?"* Jesus' response was, *"Why are you so fearful? "Don't you even yet have confidence in me?"* (TLB) He was addressing their lack of faith in Him.

At times like these, we need to examine *our* loyalty and faithfulness toward God. Most of the time we don't think that He needs or even desires our friendship, much less our loyalty. Yet, Abraham was called His friend because he believed His Word. Jesus says in John 15:15 we are no longer servants, but His friends. Isn't that wonderful to know! He wants this type of relationship with us. So, how can we be a friend to Him?

A true friendship takes place between people that have love in their hearts toward each other. Jesus Christ has shown His ultimate love in His death for us on the Cross. Even if we presently do not have love in our hearts toward Him, this love can be cultivated.

Remember how much time you spent with your special friend? The same way love occurs between two people when time is spent together communicating and learning each other's ways, a spiritual love can be developed with God. As you take time to communicate with Him and read His Word, the Holy Spirit joins your heart to God's heart. You will find yourself wanting to tell Him about your disappointments and your dreams.

A new world will open for you. You will feel loved and special! When that love relationship develops, loyalty will result. Then, if trying times take place, you will defend and praise Him in spite of what others say or what your own feelings try to dictate.

There have been times in my life when I did not understand why the prayers of others were not answered as we all had desired. Sometimes the answers to my personal prayers did not manifest right away. Some to this date are still awaiting their answer. The one main question pounds in our minds, *"Why God?" "Why wasn't the prayer*

15

answered as I had hoped?" "You certainly want it for me . . . don't you?"

Then many times, two reactions take place. One, an underlying fear settles in our spirit as to God's faithfulness to His Word and an inclination to back away emotionally from Him. We become like frightened little children who can't trust our Father as we previously thought. Many of us, at this stage, turn away from Him. We go back to our old ways and habits with an underlying sadness and even anger. We could even join the Disciples with our question, *"Don't you even care we are about to drown?"* Jesus' reply is the same to us as it was to them, ***"Don't you yet have confidence in me?"***

What must we do now? Our thoughts scream, *"Give up!" "I can't believe Him!" "I can't trust Him for my answers!"* It truly is a decision time. What must we do? We really only have one answer. We must make the decision to continue our relationship with Him. We must dig down deep within us, sometimes to our very core, and decide ***"Yes!*** *Yes, I will be your loyal friend! I do not understand, but I will trust You. Jesus, you are my hope and dreams. My life is yours."*

Then we join the Psalmist David, "I would have despaired unless I had believed that I would see the goodness of the Lord in the land of the living. Wait for the Lord; be strong, and let your heart take courage; yes, wait for the Lord." Psms. 27:13,14 (NASB)

Let us remember: A LOYAL FRIEND is a prized possession!

BELIEVE FOR YOUR DREAM

"And there we saw the giants, the sons of Anak, which come of the giants: and we were in our own sight as grasshoppers, and so we were in their sight." Numbers 13:33 (KJV)

"And all the congregation lifted up their voice, and cried; and the people wept that night." Numbers 14:1 (KJV)

Have you ever had a dream that was so important it was all you thought and talked about? When you woke in the morning, it was on your mind. As your day progressed, it would constantly take over your thoughts, giving you energy, inner excitement and purpose in living. Our dreams are unlimited because we have unlimited creative imaginations.

But it seems that many times our consuming dreams come with obstacles and unexpected problems. We remember those times also; when we had to force ourselves to try 'one more time', although every fiber of our being cried, *"Stop!" "Give up!" "Forget it!"* During those intense problem times, we really had to decide if realizing our dream was worth the supreme emotional and physical effort.

Such was the case with the Israelites in the book of Numbers. Let's look at what they faced. There were over a million of them wandering through the intensely hot and dry desert. Of course, in the desert there wasn't the water, meat and vegetables they were accustomed to having in Egypt. This caused problems all by itself. Then to top everything else, giants were discovered.

We have a hard time comprehending how the giants looked. They had the most terrifying human forms the Israelites had ever seen. It is stated in 2 Samuel 21:20 of one such giant having six fingers on both hands and six toes on each foot. Their strength was amazing. They could carry a spear the size of a large beam and stood thirteen to fourteen feet tall, almost the height of a two-story building. How would you have felt?

This final obstacle made the discouraged Israelites doubt that their dream was worth the effort. As chapter fourteen vividly describes, they gave up their dreams and cried out to God in total defeat. They had endured the lack of necessities but now believed God's promised land was unreachable and even wanted to return to the people that had enslaved them.

God knew they believed in the strength of the giants instead of in the strength of His promises, and as Numbers 14:23 records, it was at this time

He declared they would not enter the land.

We can see this from different perspectives. One point of view; since God had shown them His miracles repeatedly, He was angry for their lack of trust in Him. After all, they witnessed the miracles that set them free from Egypt, the parting of the Red Sea as well as His provision in the desert and other mighty acts of power from the glorious hand of God. So what happened? We think, *"After all God had done for them, why couldn't they believe? If we saw all those powerful miracles, we would surely believe regardless how big the giants!"* Or... would we?

Let's look a little deeper at these newly liberated slaves. Perhaps the generations of Egyptian captivity caused them to develop ingrained attitudes of defeatism, hopelessness and failure. None had ever experienced a day of personal freedom, nor did they know anyone in their family who had lived this valuable liberty. One year after another, brought more bondage. They had come to feel they could do nothing apart from their Egyptian rulers. They were helpless and did not 'feel' they could ever be overcomers or victorious.

Is it possible, with this history of defeat, their belief in the strength and size of the giants and all the horrifying fears and impossibilities, *prevented* them from putting their faith in God's ability to deliver and answer? Unfortunately, as a result of this lack of faithfulness, they wandered around in the desert until they died.

We can compare this to our lives today. We all have our dreams as did the Israelites, but do we carry with us the same attitudes of defeat, failure and hopelessness? Those things that hold us captive might be disabling mental enslavements of experiences ranging from the painful loss of a loved one, to childhood abuse, to broken marriages, to drug and alcohol addiction. These and other experiences can form our attitudes about life.

If we were raised in dysfunctional families, we may have unexplained fears and apprehensions. Often we pass on the positive or negative treatment we received as children to others - especially our own children. If we were judged, we judge. If we were criticized, we criticize. If we were hated, we hate. But also, if we were loved, we love.

Our giants may take the form of sickness, lack of opportunities, or overwhelming debt. They tower over us making us feel weak and helpless. At times we may feel like crying out in total defeat. Let us learn from the mistakes of God's chosen people and believe in Him for our answer.

We have two choices: will we believe God because of His miracles and His promise-filled Word, or will we believe in our giants? Although our experiences may make it hard for us to trust and believe in others, we can begin with trusting our heavenly Father. He is looking now, as then, to see if we will believe 'them' or Him. He has more love and kindness for us than we can ever imagine. As we trust Him, we can have confidence He will direct our steps out of the wilderness and into the joyful fulfillment of our dreams.

Let us remember: When you trust in God's faithfulness, you can BELIEVE FOR YOUR DREAM.

CHOCOLATE-COVERED CHERRIES

"Delight yourself in the Lord and he will give you the desires of your heart." Ps. 37:4 (NIV)

"*He will give you the desires of your heart*" reminds me of a precious time I had with the Lord.

When my husband and I started our advertising business, we found we had to be quite conservative with our finances. We no longer had the consistent, reliable paycheck we had grown accustomed to while he was employed as a commercial artist. Our eyes were also opened to a new world of taxes, insurance and expenditures for the business that constantly seemed to drain the monies we received. We felt if we could just "get over the hump" we would eventually make it.

Although we were willing to do whatever necessary for our new business to progress, our two young children didn't understand the sacrifices. They wanted to be like any children their age and their many needs and desires for the latest toy or clothing and our inability to fulfill their desires made me feel guilty. Knowing our budget must be followed closely, I sadly had to say *"No"* to their pleading looks and those entreating words, *"Can I have this, Mommy?"* During this intense time, we learned that the Lord is our provider in many ways we had not known. What we experienced has stayed with us to this day.

One such occasion involved chocolate-covered cherries. During one of my weekly visits to the grocery, I noticed a large display of boxed chocolate-covered cherries. As I passed the display each time I went down a different aisle, the cherries seemed to get creamier and more luscious, capturing my full attention. Pretty soon, I could even taste them. Realizing our budget could not accommodate even little extras, I forced myself not to weaken, refusing to look at them. Although I did not look however, I still remembered.

As I continued my shopping, I sighed with a deep longing and quietly whispered, *"Lord, I wish I had a box of those cherries."* I finished my shopping and by the time I put the groceries away at home and involved myself with other details of the business, I forgot the whole incident.

The next morning I received a telephone call from a friend who had a garden and wanted to bring over fresh produce. I accepted gratefully. She showed me luscious green beans, ripe red tomatoes and other delicious vegetables. As I was mentally preparing them for dinner, she reached again into her bag saying, *"I don't know if you would be interested, but I had this in my freezer and wondered if you would like it."* She then pulled out a box of (you guessed it) the creamiest looking chocolate-covered cherries, just like those at the grocery! I

was so delighted! The candied fruit was a treat, but the knowledge that the Lord had heard my whispered desire thrilled me.

From that time on, I realized He is our loving Father who listens to all our requests - large and small. I didn't have to say *"No"* to all my children's requests, but I could pray and believe He would also meet their desires. We began to pray as a family for our various needs and rejoiced in His answers; from braces for crooked teeth, to prom dresses!

Our prayers have changed over the years to include college tuition, new cars and even a Hawaiian vacation, with each answered prayer bringing its own miracle. I have also had times of struggling with stressful marital difficulties, anxious occasions of sickness in the family and despairing personal conflicts. During these times, the memory of the Lord hearing my whispered desire has comforted and sustained me. I am still warmed with the remembrance of the time I delighted myself in Him, and He gave me the desire of my heart - even a box of chocolate-covered cherries.

Let us remember: No request is too small, not even CHOCOLATE-COVERED CHERRIES!

"A cheerful heart
is good medicine,
but a crushed spirit
dries up the bones."

Proverbs 17:22 (NIV)

CORRUPT
COMMUNICATIONS

"Let no corrupt communication proceed out of
your mouth, but that which is good to the use of
edifying, that it may minister grace unto the
hearers." Ephesians 4:29 (KJV)

"*H*ello, Sara Irvine? This is Constance Marie.*
Well, I just wanted to tell you about my
horrible day. I guess you get tired of hearing from
me but, it's been one of 'those' days again. First off, I felt
just lousy when I got up this morning. I didn't sleep a
wink all night. I tossed and turned the whole night and
couldn't eat a thing this morning. So, guess what, I
ended up getting one of my horrible headaches again!
You know, the ones that feel like my head is coming
apart. I knew I would. It always happens! Anyway, I
managed to eat a bite and thought I would try to sleep
again. You know what happened next? My stupid
neighbor decided to mow his grass. Can you imagine? I
know he did it on purpose. I don't know what I will do.
I also heard the weather report say we are going to have
really bad weather. You know rain, hail, lightning and
stuff. Lightning will probably hit our houses knowing
our luck. I hate rain. It always rains this time of the year*

and I just hate it! I don't know what I'm going to do. Oh yes, I read we are all supposed to have a huge tax increase. The government is so lousy and corrupt. I also opened my mail this morning and sure enough my utilities are all going up. It is just greed. Everybody is so greedy! Sara? Are you there? Anyway, I found out termites are infesting our neighborhood. They'll probably get to our houses soon and cost us thousands of dollars. I don't know what I will do! Well, Sara, I'm tired so I guess I'll go for now. I better get some sleep if my stupid neighbor is finished. You sure are quiet. Have a good day if you can. Bye!" (click)

We sigh and stare at the telephone receiver in our hand. We somehow don't feel very well ourselves after hearing Constance Marie this morning. We kind of feel like we are getting a headache and need to go to bed. Have you ever been afraid to ask someone how they were feeling because you knew they would tell you?

"Let no corrupt communication proceed out of your mouth, but that which is good to the use of edifying, that it may minister grace unto the hearers." This is an interesting scripture considering the previous conversation. Although this exact conversation did not happen to us, we've had others like it. Two very important words to note in this scripture are 'corrupt' and 'grace'. The definition of corrupt is, "Immoral or perverted, rotting, petrified, debased by changes or errors." "Let no *corrupt* communication proceed out of your mouth, . . . " Or in other words, no immoral, perverted, petrified or debased communication. Do you ever feel debased (degraded) when you listen to someone? Have you ever felt almost a feeling of 'lifelessness' after a conversation? I have. The 'rotting' or 'deadly words' seem to drain our vitality. Corrupt communication is a serious matter with life changing consequences.

But, let's look at the rest of the scripture. ". . . but that which is good to the use of edifying, that it may minister *grace* unto the hearers." The definition of 'grace' is, "beauty or harmony of motion, form or manner, any attractive quality." What a difference! Many times we do not realize the vital importance of our communications. Let's ask ourselves, do our conversations edify and bring grace to others? It is so easy to talk of fears, problems, illness or other people's faults and weaknesses. These type of words are just the opposite of what brings grace (beauty, attractiveness, uplifting) to those that hear them.

Speaking with the well-being of others in mind takes us out of our world of *self*-preoccupation. To do this often takes much effort on our part. To constantly think and speak about ourselves and our circumstances has been ingrained in us since childhood. Children usually concentrate all their thoughts on their lives and their surroundings. If you listen to their conversations, each one tries to dominate the time with things concerning their lives

DO YOURSELF A FAVOR

and feelings. (Sounds like Constance Marie.) First Corinthians 13:11 tells us, "When I was a child, I talked like a child, I thought like a child, I reasoned like a child. When I became a man, I put childish ways behind me." (NIV) Perhaps it's time for us to join with the Apostle Paul and put away 'childish things'. One 'childish thing' to definitely put away is corrupt communications!

We will eventually speak about whatever our minds dwell on - good or bad. God's word is no exception to this rule. The more we dwell in Him and His Word, the more like Jesus we become. His Word always encourages us to be like Christ, who put His thoughts and attention on others. He said only what the Father told Him to say, - words of edification and hope. Our faithful God helps us to break the habitual cycle of negativity and cynicism. We can pray, *"Father, I speak negative words that do not bring encouragement and hope to others or myself. Please forgive me and enable me to speak only uplifting words of grace. Thank you I can be a new, edifying person."*

Now we understand more about 'corrupt' communications. We know we are to have attractive, uplifting words of encouragement and praise for others. We can apply Ephesians 4:29 today at work, home or on the telephone.

*"Hello, Sara Irvine, this is Constance Marie. I have **wonderful, exciting** news for you today! You will be so glad I called. You are such a special friend. Just listen to this!*

Let us remember: We should not speak CORRUPT COMMUNICATIONS but rather attractive words of grace to the hearers.

*Fictional names

"DO YOURSELF A FAVOR"

"And the second is like it: 'Love your neighbor as yourself.' Matthew 22:39 (NIV)

"*Oh brother, I look like I've been run over by a truck!*"

We all have days of looking at ourselves in the mirror and saying *"Blechhh!"*. An occasional spoken word of self-disapproval has been expressed by most of us, especially after a time of illness, stress or lack of sleep. However, when self-disapproval dominates our time until our mindset becomes one of perpetual dissatisfaction, we have to re-examine ourselves. Do we constantly put ourselves down and compare ourselves to others? Does everyone else seem more attractive, with much more to offer?

The world places much emphasis on appearance. The movies, commercials, billboards and advertisements make it hard for us to be objective about ourselves, causing us to fall into the trap of comparison. Our physical inadequacies seem to become increasingly pronounced, as we are pulled into the world's system of value and worth. If we don't have perfectly straight teeth, shining full hair, sleek, firm bodies, and radiant, youthful skin, we are somehow inadequate - a failure. Of course looks alone aren't enough, we must also drive the right car, live in fine homes, take fabulous vacations, plus obtain professional degrees or again, we have failed. This trap of self-preoccupation draws us away from God's admonition to love ourselves. David exclaimed in praise that he was " . . . fearfully and wonderfully made; . . ." Psalms 139:14 (NIV)

What does "love ourselves"mean? People consider having love for ourselves to be a sign of pride and self-pride is frowned upon. The admonition is not for us to have pride in our accomplishments and esteeming ourselves better than others, but to appreciate God's goodness to us. When we love the life He has given us, we show appreciation for His gift of life. Just as we want our children to appreciate the gifts we give them, the Lord desires the acknowledgment of His giving to us. We need to love and accept the lives we have received from Him. Out of this acceptance comes love for others. It is hard to love our neighbor as ourselves - as Matthew exhorts - when we don't appreciate and love His gift to us.

We all have been ensnared with thinking less of ourselves. This reveals a lack of appreciation of our Father's gift of life. I remember the morning I heard the words "do yourself a favor." I was looking in the mirror analyzing my facial flaws and said my usual *"Blechhh!"* It was then I heard a voice within me say, *"Why don't you accept yourself?"* This startled me! Ceasing to look at myself, I said, *"Lord, are you talking to me?"* The words continued,

"Why don't you do yourself a favor and love yourself?" I knew it was the Lord gently reproving me. Saying *"Blechhh!"* about myself had become a lifestyle. One I had to break.

Inferiority normally starts in our childhoods - as it did with me. Growing up in an alcoholic family made its mark on me, complete with feelings of inadequacy and shame. As with most children of dysfunctional parents, I took on their unacceptance and felt unacceptable and inferior. There are thousands of people raised in dysfunctional (not just alcoholic) families who have never heard the priceless words of praise, encouragement and approval. This leaves us feeling inadequate about our worth and attractiveness. Although we become adults, the child still lives within us with its inferior feelings. Often it is such a child that says *"Blechhh!"* about him or herself. We basically have allowed ourselves to be held captive by our childhoods.

So what can we do? The good news is Jesus has come to ". . . bind up the brokenhearted, to proclaim liberty to the captives, and the opening of the prison to them *that are bound"*. Isaiah 61:1 (KJV) The child within us no longer has to feel unloved and inferior.

That morning I pondered His "do yourself a favor" words and asked His forgiveness for my lack of acceptance of myself. Then I asked healing for the aching child within me. I determined to not speak disapproving words of myself again, but to replace them with words of acceptance and approval. It took a while to break the habit of

31

negative speaking and it is an ongoing process today. But each time I am successful, I am closer to "liberty to the captives!"

We all can receive healing by praying *"Lord, thank you for dying so that I can be healed and delivered from my hurts of the past. Please heal the child within me so I can be the victorious, confident child you want me to be. I determine to not speak, think, or act on negative words about myself, but rather words of acceptance. I rely on your strength to alter my behavior. Thank you for healing and binding up my captive heart."*

It may be hard to alter our thinking and begin to see our value and worth. But, we can do it when we realize it gives Him pleasure for us to love and accept ourselves and the gift of life He has given us. We must begin today. We will have another opportunity tomorrow morning when we look in the mirror.

Let us remember: DO YOURSELF A FAVOR; love yourself and the life you have received from Him.

DON'T LOOK TOO LONG!

"And he said, *'Come'*. And when Peter was come down out of the ship, he walked on the water, to go to Jesus. But when he saw the wind boisterous, he was afraid; and beginning to sink, he cried, saying *Lord, save me.*" Matthew 14:29-30 (KJV)

Many of us have experienced what happened to Peter in the book of Matthew. No, we haven't walked on water, but we have tried something new and weren't successful. Why is that significant? We, and Peter, looked too *long*. What do I mean? Let's look into these valuable writings from God's Word closer.

In the scriptures, Peter actually started to walk on the water but when he saw the wind 'boisterous' (violent), he became afraid and started to sink. The miracle of walking on the water is non-contested. However, there may be more we can glean from this challenging event in Matthew.

Peter, an experienced fisherman, had already experienced the violent wind. Earlier in verse 24 it states their ship was tossed with waves. But, what was different this time? Let's look at one word in Matthew, verse thirty, that suggests a reason for Peter's downfall and perhaps ours as well. He *saw* the wind! Why is that important? Could it be that he saw the wind differently than before? He now saw it as a tremendous obstacle, one of danger and overwhelming power. Once that took hold in his mind, he became afraid and began to sink.

We must remember, Peter was a professional fisherman accustomed to the sea and knew what to do with tumultuous waves. Yet, when he was actually walking on them, it was an *untried setting*. Here it is! He **saw** the wind in an **untried setting**. He had never walked on water before! It's the 'untried settings' that place us in vulnerable situations. None of us want to feel ill-equipped and vulnerable.

So, what do we do with the boisterous winds and untried settings in *our* lives? As with Peter, we begin to believe for miracles (step out in the water) and make progress until we start to *see* the waves of obstacles and our helplessness. It's the waves that try to get us to forget who is holding us up. Satan, like a roaring lion, (1 Peter 5:8) screams at us in the winds, "**Look** how hard it is! **See** how impossible it looks!" We *look too long*, fear leaks into us and then we begin to sink.

We each have our 'untried settings'. Each miracle is new and different. Although God has performed miraculously in our lives previously, our new requested miracle is an untried setting. The winds seem to blow louder and harder than ever before attempting to blow away the memory of God's previous faithfulness!

What do we do? It is at this time, we need to reaffirm ourselves with Jesus' faithful promises, calm ourselves against the raging fear and doubt by trusting and speaking continually His blood bought promises. When the thoughts rush in that we will fail or we don't have enough faith, resist them immediately and stay persistent with God's unchanging Word. The peace and calm may not always come instantly or even quickly, but they will come. Even though the wind and water may still thrash at us, we press forward in our walk.

When we step out on the waters of life, there will be 'untried settings'; however, *our Lord* is not untried! He never forsakes us and will hold our hand in the wind. We can trust Him with our lives. He is still saying, *"Come."*

Let us remember: To keep from sinking, DON'T LOOK TOO LONG!

"Pleasant words
are a honeycomb,
sweet to the soul
and healing to the bones."

Proverbs 16:24 (NIV)

"DON'T SEND ME
ANY FLOWERS"

"A word fitly spoken is like apples of gold in pictures of silver." Proverbs 25:11 (KJV)

I remember when I was a child my mother saying, *"Don't send me any flowers after I'm gone"*.

I didn't quite understand the true meaning of her words at the time. Since becoming an adult, however, I see their value. In other words she meant, *"Any kind gestures, words or actions you may have for me, show me now while I can enjoy them. Don't wait until I'm gone."*

Praise and encouragement are two of our most basic needs. From childhood to old age, we cry out for such affirmation. Since there is so much negative conduct, it is rare to receive or even to give genuine praise. We only need to watch the nightly news to see the tragic ways people behave toward each other. Of course, we all have our own stories of the rude people we have encountered.

"A word fitly spoken is like apples of gold in pictures of silver" denotes words of kindness, compassion and love. These "apples" form beautiful pictures in the lives of others. The words blossom into wonderful gardens of emotional, fragrant flowers of love, security and peace.

Unfortunately, when loved ones are gone - through moving away or death - we remember the flowers not given to them. Often this brings intense remorse. When someone is no longer with us because of death, we normally recall the good things about them. Their shortcomings do not seem as important as they once did.

A few years ago I attended the funeral of a family friend. I listened as two or three people spoke of the sacrificial things he had done for others. Others spoke of his devotion to his family. They were deserving words about a fine man with which I totally agreed!

Then I remembered my mother's words, *"Don't send me any flowers after I'm gone."* I had to ask myself, *"Did I ever tell him what a good person I thought he was for his devotion and sacrifice for others?" "Did I slow my life down enough to even notice his kind gestures?"* Sadly, I realized I had not. I should have given him fragrant flowers in the form of edifying, encouraging words so he could have enjoyed them here and now.

There have been other times I did not give verbal flowers when I should have. As with most families, children have their squabbles. My brother and I were not exceptions. We were two years apart in age and, although we loved each other, we argued regularly while growing up. Most of us think our loved ones will always be with us and we take for granted our time with them. We say or do things in anger thinking we will 'work things out' later. For me, 'later' was too late.

The night before my brother left on a trip, we argued. I do not remember the reason for the argument. It does not matter to me now. Both of us were angry and said unkind, spiteful things to each other - words I would remember for years. He never returned for us to 'work things out'. While driving in Illinois, he was hit by a truck and killed. My grief was beyond words! I could not mention his name or look at his picture for years.

Oh, the verbal flowers I wished I had said before he left! It took many years before I could forgive myself. It was only after I was born again - through believing in Jesus Christ - that I received forgiveness and healing for what I had done. Then, and only then, could I finally work through my pain.

The *"Don't send me any flowers after I'm gone"* expression from my Mother planted a new resolve within me. I make sure to tell others of their value and see their qualities, especially my family. I still have regrettable times of anger and irritation, but I try to remember her words and alter my behavior to see the good in those around me. When others act or look differently than myself, I try not to judge knowing each of us has our own story of lifes' experiences of pain and joy.

There are many people with similar experiences that only God can heal. They must receive His forgiveness and make their own resolve to see the qualities in others and tell them of their value and worth. They never know if they will see them again.

We all have bouquets of words we can plant in

39

the hearts of the people with whom we share our days. There may be those in our families or even strangers needing an encouraging message. A tender, verbal 'rose' can be spoken showing love and thankfulness for someone's kindness. Delicate words whispered like soft, gentle 'lilies' can express sympathy in times of grief or sorrow. Resounding words depicting hardy, vibrant 'pansies' congratulating someone's patience and endurance are always appreciated. Expressive, cheerful words as colorful 'daisies' can be given for the happy and pleasant attitude of someone. Within these expressive flowering words is enclosed delicate 'baby's breath' to reinforce the treasures their lives are to us.

These endearing expressions of thankfulness, sympathy and love will continue to bud into new blossoms throughout their lifetimes. Kind words, gentle hugs and helping hands can make this a beautiful place to live!

Let us remember: "DON'T SEND ME ANY FLOWERS" after I'm gone. Send some flowers today!

DRAW THE LINE

"Moses answered the people, 'Do not be afraid. Stand firm and you will see the deliverance the Lord will bring you today. The Egyptians you see today you will never see again. *The Lord will fight for you*; you need only to be still." Exodus 14: 13,14 (NIV)

The Israelites were admonished to fear not, stand still and see the Lord's salvation. What were they up against? In the preceding verses in Exodus, the scriptures describe Israel's exodus (departure) from Egypt and the armies of Pharaoh's pursuit of them. Verses ten through twelve show God's chosen people to be extremely fearful for their lives, even wanting to return to their captors. Moses proclaims to the frightened Israelis to stop fearing, stand, and see God's salvation for them. No easy task.

Let's consider their situation. The Jewish people saw the massive armies of Pharaoh arrayed in their shiny, indestructible armor. They could hear the chariots being pulled by the swift, sleek and powerful Egyptian horses. Probably seeing and smelling the dust for miles, their fear must have been paralyzing; the noise and confusion, deafening.

41

The purpose of the pursuit was either to take them back to Egypt as slaves or kill them. In the midst of this calamity, Moses boldly proclaims God will deliver them. It was a lot for the Israelites to believe. They had to in effect "draw the line" on their fears in the middle of heart-stopping panic! Why were they to stand still and not fear? Verse fourteen tells us. *"The Lord shall fight for you . . ."*

The same verses apply to us today. We are to fear not, stand and see the salvation of the Lord in our lives. Salvation includes redemption, deliverance, healing and prosperity. The words in Exodus might seem easy but application takes effort, courage and His enabling. In effect, we also have to 'draw the line' on our fears, anxiousness and doubts in the midst of our battles.

We have many illustrations of drawing the line. Remember, as children, when two boys would fight? The bully, after shoving the other boy around for a while would draw a line. He would defiantly yell to his opponent, *"Step across the line if you really mean what you say! If you have the guts!"* At that time, the challenged boy would have to decide if he really meant everything he said he would and could do. He also knew once he stepped across the line, he had to make the decision to win. Isn't it interesting how everyone looking on would wait to see if the challenged boy would step across the line? Most likely there would be silence as he made his decision.

Although we are older, life still demands the stepping across 'the line.' There are times when the 'bullies' of fear, anxiety and doubt scream out the potential for failure, sickness and defeat. When we listen to them, we waver between God's Word and their taunts. Just as the Israelites, we look at the enemies and then to the word of the Lord, while their fear-filled taunts yell at us. If we heed them, rather than the 'still small voice' of the Lord, we can fall into faithlessness. It is also interesting to note the silence as the forces of Heaven and Hell watch as we make our decision. The book of Hebrews tells us we are ". . . surrounded by such a great cloud of witnesses. . ." Hebrews 12:1

We have to 'draw the line', not as the bully in the illustration, but as a victorious Christian. How do we do it? We say, *"Enough is enough!" "I'll have no more!" "My God will fight for me!"*

43

This line can be a literal line impression on carpeting, a chalk mark on the floor or even a mental assessment. However, one side of the line encompasses the fears and doubts of the enemy and the other side represents faith and victory in our God.

Just as the challenged boy had to summon up courage, we need to remember God's Word to be strong and very courageous. We must believe the salvation of the Lord is with us as we step across the line - to victory! The best way to equip ourselves for this battle is to memorize those verses in scripture that remind us of God's promises and His absolute power to fulfill them. Moses admonition to the Israelites applies to us, *"The Lord will fight for you!"*

Let us remember: There will be times we will need to DRAW THE LINE and step across it to victory.

FROM THE SERIES
LET US REMEMBER

EMPTY YOUR POCKETS!

"Cast your cares on the Lord and he will sustain you; he will never let the righteous fall."
Psalm 55:22 (NIV)

"Cast all your anxiety on him because he cares for you." 1 Peter 5:7 (NIV)

M ost of us know what it's like to accumulate change in our pockets throughout the day. Before retiring for the evening or just relaxing, we empty our pockets. We normally put our change on the night stand or bathroom counter and hang up our clothes. It becomes a habitual part of our lives and we don't think much about it.

But, do you know there are other pockets that get filled during the day? We don't notice these pockets because we can't feel physical weight in them and they don't make a jingling sound when we walk. However, these filled 'pockets' determine our day's attitudes and dispositions. Are we still talking about change? Yes and no.

As we go about our daily activities of work, relationships with our families and others with whom we come in contact, we accumulate an assortment of 'mental change'. This mental change

45

doesn't weigh us down physically but, most assuredly, weighs us down emotionally. An unkind remark can come in the size of a penny or nickel. *"You don't look very good in that outfit!"* *"What has happened to your hair!"* *"Have you gained weight?"* An attack on our work performance can be the dimension of a dime or quarter. *"You're not performing on your job as well as you should!"* *"A computer can replace your job!"* *"You might get fired!"* A family disturbance can take on proportions of a half dollar. *"I want to run away from home!"* *"No one understands me!"* *"I want a divorce!"*

As too much change could stress or tear a cloth

46

pocket, the mental change in our minds becomes heavier and heavier, causing all kinds of distress. Scientific studies have been conducted indicating that depression and anxiety are on the increase affecting all ages. Other studies strongly suggest that harboring anger and negative emotions releases chemicals that build up in our system, becoming toxic over time.

Jesus has said to *cast our anxiety and cares* on Him. Is it possible He knows the deadly effects of negative mental accumulation? Of course He does! He said in John 14:27, "Peace I leave with you; my peace I give you. I do not give to you as the world gives. Do not let your hearts be troubled and do not be afraid." In effect, we are to empty our mental pockets (casting our cares) by placing our regrets, angers, disappointments and fears in His hands. This is so very needful in our anxious, stress-filled days.

Just as we clean out the pockets of our garments at night, let us clean out our minds of the worries and problems of the day. How do we do this? First, take a few moments at night and get by yourself. (Use the bathroom if it is the only place that's empty.) Next, close your eyes and take a deep breath and release it out slowly. Then say, *"Jesus, I give these burdens, the negative mental change, to you. I know you care for me and my mental health. I forgive _____ for the unkind remarks. I give my fears and concerns to you. Please take care of them. I don't know how You will work them out, but I trust You will. Thank you, Lord, for hearing and answering my prayers."*

47

He will hear and answer your prayers and you will sleep much better, feeling more rested the next morning. Remember, we accumulate a lot of different kinds of change during the day so don't forget to clean out **all** your pockets tonight!

Let us remember: When you feel mentally weighed down, EMPTY YOUR POCKETS!

FOUR MORE YARDS

"Do you not know that in a race all the runners run, but only one gets the prize? Run in such a way as to get the prize." 1 Corinthians 9:24 (NIV)

While in high school my husband, a running back in football, developed an interesting battle strategy for victory. While on the playing field, during each play he focused all his strength and attention on gaining at least four yards. In so doing, if there was no fumble, he knew his team would score the touchdown. He did not look at the obstacles between himself and the goal line because there were so many variables. So, as he recounted to me, he would 'put his head down' and forge ahead thinking of only those four yards. If he got more yardage, (which often he did), that was great, but he resolved to get at least those four. This strategy resulted in victory for their team. During this time of intense concentration, he never allowed himself to see the impossibilities but only concentrated on those "four more yards".

This principle can be applied to all walks of life. For example, let's say, a person begins college as a first-year student to become a doctor. If he or she were to see all the obstacles between them and the

goal, they would more than likely lose heart. They have to see themselves as future doctors, but concentrate on one semester at a time. In effect, they have to 'put their heads down', forge ahead and make "four more yards"! A teacher, salesperson, musician, author, business man or woman, parent, spouse etc., all have the same four more yard's principle.

Business people can only be as successful as the day before them. Each successful day eventually results in a rewarding, fulfilling career. Parents can only take 'one day at a time' in raising their children. Each new day brings the variableness and unpredictability of their children's individual personalities. A couple's marriage is built on a daily interaction of commitment, love and sacrifice. Each of these have to take 'four yards' at a time with each yard being played to its very best to result in success.

We often try to project the end results of success to the point that we lose our focus on the yardage before us. We want the touchdowns in life without putting forth the effort on the playing field. It will not happen. We only get as close to our goals as our immediate steps. "Four more yards" played at our best will bring our longed for touchdowns!

Let us remember: In all areas of life, concentrate on FOUR MORE YARDS!

GOING HOME

"I will set out and go back to my father and say to him: Father, I have sinned against heaven and against you." Luke 15:18 (NIV)

There may be times in our Christian walk when we drift away from the Lord. We certainly don't plan on drifting, but after a series of negative events take place, we realize we have gone away from Him. One such event happened to me. Perhaps you or someone you know can relate to my experience.

After a series of trials and offenses with several people, I found that I was not feeling the Lord's presence, nor a desire to do His work. I felt hurt and confused because of other's actions and words against me. I did not understand that my battle is not with flesh and blood (other people) but with the rulers of the darkness of this world (Eph. 6:12). Continuing to see other people and not Satan as my problem, I began to drift away from asking God to be my protector and reacted in anger to the offenses. I slowly retreated into my own world of self-justification, sure that I was right and they were wrong. So many of us have fallen into this trap.

This world of self-justification is lonely and

lacking in joy. Proverbs 14:14 indicates a Christian can backslide from God, but a backslide can be a series of 'backdrifts'. A slide is quick and deliberate, however, a backdrift is a slow almost unnoticeable change of position. We normally don't backslide from God when we have been in constant communication with Him praying and reading His word. The backdrift is much more dangerous. Things appear to be the same for a while and can lull us into a ominous complacency.

When I think of drifting, I remember being at the ocean on a raft drifting along on the water enjoying the warmth of the sun. With each gentle,

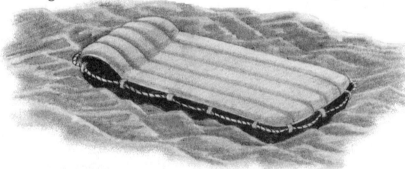

rolling movement of the waves I could feel the tension and stress ooze out of me as I slipped into a state of relaxed calm. Closing my eyes, I breathed a long sigh of contentment. After a while, I looked around and realized I drifted a very long distance down the shore from my starting point. Calm disappeared and tension quickly returned because of the effort it took to drag my raft back to the motel!

Comparing my experience on the ocean to my spiritual life; because of the hurtful things done to me and my reacting in anger, I was surprised at how far I had drifted from the Lord. Each verbal assault slowly hardened my heart toward my attackers causing a ugly coating of resentment over my heart. This coating protected me some-what from the hurt but also kept me from feeling His love as intensely. Being in His presence did not bring tears of joy to me as it had before, and my heart did not overflow with deep love for Him. He seemed to be so far away!

I had been in a relaxed state of spiritual contentment before the verbal attacks and was not prepared for what I felt was an assault by other people. I did not have on my 'spiritual armor' as Ephesians 6:13-17 so plainly teaches. Just as each wave in the ocean took me from my starting point, each offense caused my spiritual raft to drift farther and farther away from my place with the Lord.

During this experience, I knew that not all was well with me spiritually, but I let life's busyness absorb my thoughts and ignored the coolness of my heart toward the Lord. It was not until I was asked to teach a Bible study that I slowed myself down enough to seek God about my strayed condition.

Although I had drifted from God it was not obvious to other people, especially since I stayed actively involved in church activities. I still had a 'smile' on my face while the truth of hurt and resentment in my heart stayed successfully hidden from others. Realizing I had to face my condition because I had run out of excuses, I couldn't ignore my detachment from Him any longer. I also knew I desperately needed His anointing to teach the class. My experience of returning to Him will forever be ingrained in my heart and mind. Let me tell you about it.

The night before the Bible study, I knelt down in my quiet, darkened living room and poured my heart out to the Lord. Just like the prodigal son in the book of Luke, I asked forgiveness for drifting from Him, and with tears streaming down my face I asked if I could come back home to my heavenly Father. With more heart-changing tears, I forgave my offenders and asked forgiveness for those I offended. The dark living room became my own private sanctuary with the Lord. Then something wonderful happened!

In my mind, I saw myself as a young child wearing a lace dress and shining black shoes, climbing onto my heavenly Father's lap. Though I couldn't see His face, I knew it was Him. I had to pull on His long robe to climb up but He didn't seem to mind. He seemed to be patiently waiting for me. After much exertion, I finally pulled and tugged myself up onto His lap snuggling close against Him. Laying my head on His broad, robe-covered chest, I breathed a deep sigh of relief. Sitting on His lap feeling peaceful and secure, love returned to me while I was enveloped in His acceptance. The little girl in me who felt the hurt and rejection was being healed. Relief filled me, and the gratitude I felt has stayed with me to this day.

There are many people on their own spiritual rafts who do not realize how far away they have drifted from God. Many times it is the child within them that becomes offended and hurt. They just carry each hurt within their adult bodies. The hurts of the past manifest themselves in feelings of anger, judgmentalism, criticism and underlying unhappiness. I was one of those people.

As adults, when offenses come, we have a hard time understanding why we drift from God, but He knows each hurt and rejection, and He came to heal us. The sixty-first chapter of Isaiah clearly reveals His compassion for our suffering. At times like these we need to drag our 'spiritual rafts' back to Him!

The experience to which I refer above happened quite a few years ago but is still as engraved on my heart as though it were yesterday. "Going home" has a totally different meaning to me now.

Let us remember: When 'back drifting' occurs, GOING HOME brings gratefulness and love.

"The blessing of the Lord
brings wealth,
and he adds no trouble to it."

Proverbs 10:22 (NIV)

HEAR THE HISS-S-S

"Then Jesus was led up by the Spirit into the wilderness to be tempted by the devil." Matthew 4:1 (NASB)

H ave you ever wondered why Jesus, after being baptized, was led into the wilderness to be tempted by the devil? I have. To better understand, let's go back to Genesis.

The account in Genesis is a familiar story. The serpent, having a conversation with Eve, deceived her into eating from the tree of 'good and evil'. He undermined her by lying as to God's directives for she and Adam. God had explicitly commanded Adam, "... *but from the tree of the knowledge of good and evil* ***you shall not eat****, for in that day that you eat from it, you shall surely die.*" Gen. 2:16,17 (NASB) The deceived Eve did eat from the tree and Adam, being with her, received the fruit also and as a result, spiritual death occurred.

It is interesting to read in the previous scripture (vs. 15), Adam was instructed by God to 'cultivate and keep the garden'. This is a very important scripture for us to remember. What does cultivate and keep mean? The Hebrew word for keep is 'shamar' which means "to hedge about, guard,

beware and protect". The serpent's deceiving words were most assuredly used to undermine Adam's secure existence. His successful attack totally changed Adam's life and all mankind's lives after Him! At this time, sin entered the former 'sinless paradise' and the usurper Satan became the false ruler of this world.

So back to the question, "Why was Jesus led into the wilderness to be tempted by the devil?" Jesus became the second and last Adam. (1 Cor. 15:45) He redeemed humankind from the deception and rule of Satan. 1 John 3:8 tells us, "The Son of God appeared for this purpose, that He might destroy the works of the devil." (NASB) Jesus was not deceived by the lies of Satan and His mission was a complete victory. He took away Satan's control and totally defeated him!

Now all Satan can do is to *deceive* humankind into believing he, the enemy, has control and not God. This is done by what worked in the beginning of Genesis with Eve, LIES! Lies involving defeat, worthlessness, fear and discord will be whispered into the minds of men and women.

When we accept Jesus Christ as our Lord and become co-heirs with Him (Rom. 8:16,17), thereby breaking away from Satan's rule, we become like 'mini Adams' ourselves. The same responsibilities face us that faced Adam. We have the 'garden' of our lives to cultivate and protect. However, if we do not know our responsibilities, our lives can be filled with confusion, strife, fear, sickness, poverty and every evil work!

When Jesus proclaimed at His crucifixion, *"It is finished"*, all was completed. (John 19:30) He regained our position for rulership as the children of God. Because of His ultimate life-giving sacrifice, we can assume our place. We have audience with God, our Father, when we come to Him in the name of Jesus. We can receive all that he did for us at the Cross which includes healing, redemption, deliverance and prosperity!

Man has been created a little lower than the angels. (Psm. 8:5) The fallen angel, Satan, has been defeated and cannot have dominion over us unless we *listen* to his enticements and lies. That sounds very much like what happened to Adam and Eve in the garden. We learn our position in the Lord by reading and meditating in His powerful, life giving Word. God's Word is our title deed to our rights purchased by Jesus.

When we "hear the hiss" of strife and discord, the hiss of fear, the hiss of confusion, sickness, poverty and sin coming toward us, we need to identify the true enemy! We often turn on others as being the source of our problems. Paul wrote, "For our struggle is not against flesh and blood, but against the rulers, against the powers, against the world forces of this darkness, against the spiritual forces of wickedness in the heavenly places." Eph. 6:12 (NASB)

So, as "mini Adams" we must recognize we also are gardeners over the most important plots of land in the world. . . our families and our lives! Let us take our spiritual 'gardening tools' of the Holy Spirit of God and protect our lands (lives) against the usurper! We have a position of victory in Christ Jesus. When we "hear the his-s-s", let's take the word of God and run him off!

Let us remember: HEAR THE HISS-S-S and keep our gardens safe!

"I HATE DIETS!"

"So whether you eat or drink or whatever you do, do it all for the glory of God."
1 Cor. 10: 31 (NIV)

Do you know we have an answer from the Word of God for our eating problems and disorders?

"What do you mean? Does it deal with dieting? 'I hate diets!' They don't work! I've dieted over and over again!"

To answer your questions, yes and no. It's not a diet, but will produce the benefits of a successful one! This concept is an entirely different way of thinking about food.

A diet normally denies us of something we desire. We want foods that usually aren't good for us; in many cases, stuff called 'junk food'. 'Junk food' did not even exist fifty years ago. Now it's a household word. But this answer, from God's Word, results in life and health to our bodies and also to our souls. It's a very simple concept that not only involves what we eat or drink, but our lifestyles.

There is so much more we can learn about dieting or, in most cases, food deprivation. *"Now, wait a minute! I am an 'authority' on diets! It seems like I have read every book on the market!"* I'm sure you have, but let's look further.

Countless books have been written on how to lose those 'extra' pounds. Most of the books produce a success plan if followed closely. We should count our calories, watch 'fat' grams, eat certain foods and even eat at certain times of the day. We also must consume plenty of fruit and vegetables, drink eight to ten glasses of water a day and exercise is essential! Whew! Then if we continue the diet 'indefinitely', we will be sleek and energetic! *"But what about the holidays, vacations, birthdays and 'blue Mondays'? These are all times to eat! We have to enjoy our holidays . . . right?"*

Yes, of course, we are to enjoy our holidays and different diet and exercise plans are beneficial and healthy. However, let's see if there is more we need to consider. What does God say? **"So whether you eat, or drink, or whatever you do, do it all for the glory of God."** Basically, this scripture sums up the walk of a Christian. It is so much more than an issue of food or drink. When we do all to the glory of God, what and how much we eat and drink or whatever we do, involves Him!

"I never thought of that before. I thought food was just something for me to enjoy!" Yes, it is. However, God's Word says that this precious commodity is to be eaten to His glory.

Our bodies are the houses of the Holy Spirit. God loves us tremendously and wants us to be well and enjoying the abundant life. His admonition to us is so much easier than diets! We may have to limit

our foods for a while as we grip the kitchen counter with white knuckles and resist the double chocolate cream cake. But, when our motivation is different, we don't have to *force* ourselves to please God. We *want* to please Him, because we love Him. We may still have to force ourselves to diet but now we have the power of our love for Him to motivate us

When our thoughts and attentions concentrate on His glory instead of ourselves and our passions, we find peace. Jesus is our example. When He spoke to the Father, He declared *"I have glorified Thee on the earth. . ."* John 17:4 (NASB)

Having the mindset to do 'all to the glory of God' requires having a relationship with Him. Attempting to live our lives without a love relationship and faith in God can bring what is called a 'law' mentality and continued failure. These feelings of failure carry guilt and condemnation. They rob us of our desire to continue altering our behavior. (Sounds very much like a diet, doesn't it?)

"What is a law mentality?" A law mentality is

one of attempting to obtain justification (right standing with and approval from God) by our works or denials. During Jesus' day, the Pharisees, a Jewish religious sect, attempted to utilize the law by using works to obtain their justification. The Apostle Paul was quick to point out in Galatians 2:16 that justification comes from God. Our flesh may cry out to have it's way, but when our love for God exceeds our passions, His glory is ever present in our minds. He will enable and freely give this love as we seek Him for it.

So, we see we do not have a 'law' mentality but a 'relationship' mentality with God. It's not how much we deny ourselves with food or drink. It's what gives *Him glory*! He wants us to enjoy the foods and drinks He has created. We simply must ask and receive His blessing. As we desire His glory, He will reveal the areas that we '*get*' to alter.

Also, the good news! He will help us to be victorious! It is a new relationship of dependency on Him. We not only receive our long sought after health and sleekness but committed, successful lifestyles as well! This truly is good news. . . because we do *hate diets!*

Let us remember: When we feel, "I HATE DIETS!", let's do all to the glory of God.

"I NEED MY LOVIN'!"

"Let us not become weary in doing good, for at the proper time we will reap a harvest if we do not give up." Galatians 6:9 (NIV)

We often do not realize how important it is to be consistent in our actions, and how often others notice our inconsistencies. We especially have to be constant in our responses while raising our children. I want to share this story in the hope of encouraging you in this area.

When my little red-haired daughter turned two years of age, she showed a surprising amount of temper. I noticed it particularly when she and her five-year-old brother played together. He often provoked her to anger - especially when he scared her with worms - but, I knew her temper had to be controlled. I especially realized it was a serious matter when she kicked him in the mouth while wearing her shiny new patent leather shoes!

Being a young mother, I knew very little about psychology or, for that matter, how to raise children. But I did what all mothers do - the best I could. (Does this sound familiar so far?)

I told my children I would not allow yelling insults or hitting by either child and promised that punishment would follow if they started fighting. I then sat them down and explained how important they were to each other, to their Mommy and Daddy and to the Lord. They seemed receptive. I then explained if they treated each other badly, they must apologize and hug each other or their negative actions could lead to a spanking. They didn't seem quite as receptive to this. My little blond haired, blue-eyed boy seemed more resistant than his sister to this ultimatum.

All went well for a day, and then the inevitable happened. The arguing and anger began again. I sternly reminded them of our previous conversation and made them apologize and hug each other. Then I held them and told them of my love and pride in them. This cycle was repeated over the next few days, each time concluding with their apologies and hugs along with my hugging them in approval.

After a time of doing these actions repeatedly, it appeared that there was no change taking place in their hearts. When they hugged each other, they were still as 'stiff as boards'. So I took them a step farther into their showing love by saying, *"You need to kiss each other on the cheek."*

This was the final straw! It was just too much to bear . . . an apology, a hug and now a *kiss!* They widened their eyes in astonishment with the unspoken thoughts, *"How can you possibly expect **that** of me?"* This was followed by what I can best describe as contorted faces and gagging sounds of total disgust that can only be done by children that age.

Overlooking their subhuman gestures, I restated

the consequences of not obeying. They very reluctantly conceded. Having to be consistent was most assuredly taxing for me. However, each time they conquered their own wills with these expressions of love, I hugged and spoke praise to them. I thought, *"Will this ever work?"* and prayed I was doing the right thing since I wasn't seeing any change in their attitudes.

One hectic day, they got into a verbal fight again. I was very busy, but I took the time to take them through their steps and watched them hug and kiss each other. However, I rushed away, leaving out a very, very important step.

They stayed still and didn't move. This was very unusual, since they normally would race off to play after our routine of hugs and praises. When I turned around, wondering why they were still standing there; my little girl, with all the intensity she could muster, waved her small tightly clenched fists up and down and exclaimed very dramatically, *"I need my lovin'!"*

I looked down at her beseeching blue eyes and then at her brother's similarly questioning look. They were no longer upset with each other; now their attention was on my meeting their need for love and approval. I felt my heart turn over with love for these precious little people. The fatigue and time schedule melted away. The most important thing in the world at that moment was to meet their need.

I knelt down, pulled them to me and hugged them very closely. Closing my eyes, I wanted this moment to last forever. However, it was over all

67

too quickly. They hugged me back and, once again satisfied and secure, raced off to play. I knew then that the consistency had indeed paid off, that the change of hearts was taking place! The realization also penetrated to the core of my heart of how vital love and praise were, and still are to them.

Their arguments diminished over the years, and today as young adults they still apologize, hug and occasionally kiss each other on the cheek. People remark about how much they seem to care and show respect for each other. When asked why they treat each other this way, their reply is, *"Mom wouldn't let us be mean to each other."* They are no longer 'stiff as boards' when they express their apologies because their hearts have been changed by God's grace and love.

My fiery little two-year-old daughter has grown into a fine young woman and is pursuing her Masters' degree in Developmental Child Psychology - now I can learn from her! But, you know, although she is grown, I find she still needs her *'lovin'*, her praise and acceptance.

Let us remember: When it doesn't appear a change of heart is taking place in our children or others, continue to love and show praise to them. Each of us has a child inside us who feels, "I NEED MY LOVIN'!"

"I NEVER GOT TO SAY GOODBYE!"

"Surely he hath borne our griefs, and carried our sorrows: yet we did esteem him stricken, smitten of God, and afflicted." Isaiah 53:4 (KJV)

"I never got to say goodbye!" Words like these are some of the most plaintive cries of an abandoned heart. I have heard them from many people during times of counseling and have even uttered them myself.

I listened as my grief-stricken friend, tears streaming down her face, expressed her sorrow when her sister passed away. She never got to tell her *'goodbye'*. What do you say?

My heart went out to an anguished mother as she told me of her only son dying in a freak skiing accident. He left healthy and strong and she never saw him again. What do you say to ease *that* kind of pain?

A middle-aged man carried his hidden grief for many years over the passing of his grandmother. She was the most important person in his young life. He wondered why he would have "unexplained" times of tears. Again, what do you say? Her death happened so many years ago.

A sullen young man demonstrated his heartbreak with anger and rebellion after his father's untimely death. His life was violently changed. What can you say that he could understand?

In my own family, my heart was pierced when my son, as a child, expressed his deep sadness because of his grandmother's death and absence. With tears overflowing his big blue eyes, he whispered in a small voice, *"I never got to say goodbye to Grandma. And, I'll never see her again!"* What could I say? There was nothing I could do, and how I wish I could have changed it. I missed her so very much.

I also felt deep remorse when my father died. Again, no chance for 'goodbyes'. The night my brother was killed in a tragic automobile accident, we had argued bitterly before he left. I not only didn't get to say *"Goodbye,"* but hard, angry words were my last remembrance. My grief was relentless. I ran from its pain for many years. What could I have done?

In each situation, from each person, the same words were spoken, ***"I never got to say goodbye!"*** There are many who have felt this type of sorrow and still suffer with its related feelings. There is no age limit. The need for us to say goodbye to those we love is of utmost importance.

There are so many questions. What do we do when they are gone and unable to hear our words? What do we do with the deep, unending ache inside? What do we do when we feel we will never be the same? What do we do with the questions that don't have answers?

It is at such times that we are the most vulnerable and in need. We feel stripped emotionally to our very core. Man cannot comfort us in our areas of pain. Only **God** can accomplish the inward healing! Only *He* can reach in and lighten our aching hearts and bring relief!

Often we will let the pain and guilt remain, carrying them around for years, as I did. Over a period of time, this pain can be buried so deep we do not realize its existence, but have an inexplicable sadness or even anger, as the middle-aged man experienced. Grief can cause emotional and physical illness. To 'bear' this grief only lessens our life and testimony.

What do we say to those with unspoken 'goodbyes'? We gently tell them, *"I can never truly understand your loss, for each person's separation is an individual experience. Although I never knew your loved one as you have, I can relate to your sorrow. But, there is hope for all of us."* We continue, *"Jesus died for our griefs and sorrows so we don't have to bear them. We have to take our words of loss to Him. We must not allow ourselves to think, 'I deserve to hurt.' You don't! Jesus wants you free."*

Jesus' healing can come to us in different ways. When a child has a need, he raises his arms to his father for comfort. We, as God's children, can reach up to our heavenly

71

Father for His soothing touch. Our unspoken 'goodbyes' can then be placed in His loving arms. We can say, *"Dear Jesus, I cannot tell _____ good-bye. You carried the sorrow I feel to the cross. I give my grief and sorrow to you so I will not bear them anymore. I forgive myself for not being with _____ before he (she) passed away. I give to you the 'goodbye' I wanted to say to _____. Please heal my pain and direct my steps toward a brighter tomorrow. Thank you, Lord, I receive your healing."*

The peace felt is sometimes instantaneous; other times, it comes more gradually. But, it will come. We must resist the former grief and reaffirm Jesus' deliverance from our sorrows. He has come to "... heal the brokenhearted... and set at liberty them that are bruised!" Luke 4:18 (KJV) His promises are forever.

Let us remember: If we say, "I NEVER GOT TO SAY GOODBYE!", lift our arms to Him.

"I'M DANCING AS HARD AS I CAN!"

"Let us not become weary in doing good, for at the proper time we will reap a harvest if we do not give up." Galatians 6:9 (NIV)

D o you feel like you are doing all you can do and even more is required of you?

I've felt that way. Many of us do. With both husbands and wives working, along with raising their families and attending to social functions, they feel pushed to the limit. They could say an expression I've often heard, *"I'm dancing as hard as I can!"* Only in their situation they could say, *"We are dancing as hard as we can!"*

The full time college students holding down full time jobs feel, *"I can't do anything more!"* They are 'dancing as hard as they can'.

The single parents struggling to make ends meet plus taking care of the emotional and physical needs of their children feel unable to do 'one thing more'. They also are 'dancing as hard as they can'.

The caring pastors of churches with all the many diversities and needs of the people plus trying to juggle enough time for their own families needs are overwhelmed at times. Their cry is, *"I want to help more, but, 'I'm dancing as hard as I can!"*

This expression can also be used in other areas. Those individuals struggling with the mental stresses of excessive debt are often overwhelmed. The desire to be free of the debt's oppressive weight is relentless. They think daily, *"How can I finally be free of this burden! It seems like for every step I take forward in getting out of debt, I get knocked back two steps by an unexpected financial crises!"* Again, more people also feeling the same as the others, 'dancing as hard as they can'.

There can be many illustrations. Paul's encouragement in Galatians applies to us today as it did when it was written. "Let us not become weary in doing good. . ." Even though these areas are truly dramatic and taxing, there is another important area, other than those mentioned above, to which this exhorting can apply.

As we grow in the Lord, we know we are to be transformed in His image of love. We find the admonishment in 1 Cor. 13: 4,5,7 stating that love is patient, kind, envies not, does not boast and is not proud. It is not rude or self-seeking nor easily angered and does not keep a record of wrongs. Also, love always protects, trust, hopes and perseveres.

74

Even though our hearts desire is to do the Lord's will, these admonitions seem an impossible task at times! We especially feel this way when we are experiencing the exhaustion of the stresses mentioned above. There are 'opportunities' daily to apply the principles in the thirteenth chapter of Corinthians.

A family relationship requires a special ability for patience. The children go through constant changes from emotional, hormonal to 'growing spurts'! As we direct our children on the paths they are to travel, our desires are to be examples of the Lord to them which means we try to apply the 'love chapter' daily.

The marriage of a man and woman necessitates a transformation from the life of one person to the lives of two. This conversion involves constant change and blending.

While we associate with fellow employees and employers, we have to keep in our minds that our first job assignment is to be Christians. We must represent God wherever we go and whatever we do. Again, 1 Corinthians and Galatians 6:9 applies to each area.

The ability to represent Christ requires His enabling. When we place ourselves in submission to Him, He gives us the strength, grace and power. The scripture stating to "not be weary in doing good" indicates we can have weariness during this time of growth. It would not have been written if it did not occur.

At times when weariness is present, this is where the saying applies, ***"I'm dancing as hard as***

I can!" In other words, *"I'm trying to adjust, change, blend, represent and be an example as fast as I'm able!"* This is not saying we should give up or that we will not continue to grow. It just means we tell ourselves to be patient as we are being transformed.

We must remember that we *will* reap that which we are seeking and to not give up. With our lives of activity and constant change, let us not be discouraged with the speed of our growth or fail to forgive our shortcomings. We really are *"dancing as hard as we can!"*

Let us remember: When we feel weary, we can say "I'M DANCING AS HARD AS I CAN!"

IN DUE SEASON

"And he shall be like a tree planted by the rivers of water, that bringeth forth his fruit **in his season**: his leaf also shall not wither: and whatsoever he doeth shall prosper." Psalms 1:3 (KJV)

"And let us not be weary in well doing: for **in due season** we shall reap, if we faint not." Galatians 6:9 (KJV)

W hen I was younger, I remember my Mom saying *"In due season, Frieda, everything* in *due season."*

She normally stated these words of wisdom when I was impatiently waiting for something to occur. My despairing questions at the time seem amusing to me now. *"When will I grow taller? "When can I start dating?" "When will I ever graduate?"* Her wise words frustrated me since, although I knew they were true, they meant I had to continue to wait.

Since then, I've learned to take those words more seriously. So many occasions in our lives require times of patiently waiting for answers to our prayers. Negative employment conditions, spouses or children away from God, lingering sicknesses, to name a few, stretch our faith to continue believing for a change and to not give up. One such time occurred with my husband, Jim.

In the early years of his employment as a commercial artist, he worked for a company whose owner was known for his extremely bad temperament. It only took my husband a short time to understand why his employer had such a negative reputation. Every Monday morning, they would have a 'planning session' in the owner's office during which time the man would yell and throw anything within hands reach!

Needless to say, my husband wanted to leave. However, since he needed a job and had a family to support, he stayed and we prayed! We forgave his employer on a daily basis. Often Jim did not feel like forgiving, but he knew he had to be obedient to God's Word. Hating his job, he prayed every day, *"God, get me out of here!"*

One day in the midst of his travailing prayer, he heard a still, small voice within him that he recognized as the Lord. *"Jim, you shouldn't be praying for yourself. You should be praying for your employer. You have the truth and are born again, but he is tormented. He does not have your peace and that is why he is behaving as he does. You should not leave until you have the victory."*

When Jim heard those words, it gave him peace to know God was very much aware of his situation; but, he still wanted to leave. We did change our prayers to include his employer's salvation but also, to give my husband the ability to overcome.

Time went on and it seemed the more we prayed the worse his employer got. To make matters worse, Jim's immediate supervisor wrongfully accused him of a business mistake that incurred the wrath of the owner even more.

The next day he called Jim into his office. After doing his usual yelling routine, he told Jim he had to leave at the end of the week. Instead of being upset that Jim was fired, we rejoiced! He could finally leave! But, what took place next showed us the reward of **"in due season"**.

Unbeknownst to my husband, during the week he completed his employment, employees in the different parts of the company waged a form of internal revolt. They individually walked into the other co-owner's office protesting Jim's dismissal and complained of the wrong doing. It looked like a mutiny!

The irate owner was informed by the co-owner of the employees protests. The next day the explosive employer called Jim into his office again. My weary husband wondered, *What is he going to do now? I'm already fired.* He very reluctantly went to his office. This time the man's attitude was entirely different. He acted mannerly and very awkwardly apologized for his former behavior. In his apology, he said he realized Jim had not made the business error and also told him of the employees protesting his dismissal. He then very sheepishly, with his head lowered, asked Jim to continue working.

Victory had come! Jim was vindicated! We knew he never could have changed his circumstances by

his own power or persuasiveness. His "due season" had arrived! After that day, his employer no longer questioned him or requested the Monday morning 'planning sessions'. Jim stayed with the company for a short time and left to start his own business. He left the company in *victory*. "And he shall be like a tree planted by the rivers of water, that bringeth forth his fruit **in his season**: his leaf also shall not wither: and whatsoever he doeth shall prosper."

"And let us not be weary in well doing... " The tendency to become weary in believing for a change in Jim's employment situation was ever present. We often felt like we couldn't hold on, but the Lord empowered us with His strength. The Greek translation of weary means "to fail in heart or faint."

Weariness and wanting to give up before the prayer is answered can often decide if we receive our answer. When we begin our walk of faith, we have the vitality and freshness of the Word in our spirits that gives us a thrust of confidence. After walking a while, without seeing or feeling the manifestation of the answered prayer and with the problem still being apparent, our tendency is to lose heart, grow weary and want to give up.

Paul would not have exhorted us this way in Galatians had the weariness not been a cycle that affects us. In our walk of faith we must recognize the cycle, reaffirm God's promises and not allow despair to get a foothold in our Spirit. "In due season", the promise will be manifested - sometimes in an instant - other times much later, but often when you least expect it!

(I know, Mom, *In due season, Frieda, everything in due season!*)

Let us remember: IN DUE SEASON we will reap the fruit of answered prayer.

"Trust in the Lord with all your
heart
and lean not on your own
understanding;
in all your ways acknowledge
Him,
and He will make your paths
straight.

Proverbs 3:5,6 (NIV)

"IS MY ARM TOO SHORT?"

"The Lord answered Moses, 'Is the Lord's arm too short? You will now see whether or not what I say will come true for you." Numbers 11:23 (NIV)

How would you like to have the responsibility of caring for over a million complaining people?

No easy task! Our families of sometimes complaining people take most of our energy. But, caring for over a million people is what Moses encountered. We can learn to respect him even more than we realized.

In the portions of scriptures in Numbers chapter eleven, the Israelites were once again complaining. This time, their complaint concerned their lack of meat to eat. When the Lord heard their discontent, He told Moses to tell the people they would eat meat not only for one day, but a whole month. Let's see how Moses reacted to these astounding words from the Lord.

"But Moses said, 'Here I am among six hundred thousand men on foot, and you say, 'I will give them meat to eat for a whole month!' Would they have enough if flocks and herds were slaughtered for them? Would they have enough if all the fish in the sea were caught for them?" Numbers 11:21,22 Or, in today's vernacular, Moses might have said, *"Say what?"*

What would we have done? We must remember this all occurred in a hot, dry desert where there was barely enough water for survival much less an abundance of fish or wildlife. Even after Moses had seen many other glorious miracles, he questioned the Lord. There were over 600,000 footmen (hearty eaters) not counting the thousands of other woman and children. He could not *see* how, in the desert, they would receive enough to feed them all.

We can relate to his concern. Although we experience God's miracles, when a situation arises that seems impossible to us, we also question God. We can't *see* how He can answer our requests.

After Moses expressed his dismay, God asked him the question. *"Is my arm too short or powerless to fulfill My Word?"* What a question and what a response by God in answer to Moses' need! "Now a wind went out from the Lord and drove quail in from the sea. It brought them down all around the camp to about three feet above the ground, as far as a day's walk in any direction."

Numbers 11:31 (NIV) The people killed quail for two days, amounting to **millions** of birds. Truly a miracle! We, as well as Moses, would never have solved the mystery of how God would provide. BUT, HE DID!

Today the Lord is still asking the question of us, *"Is my arm too short?"* Our requests may not be as huge as supplying food for over a million people but, sometimes our petitions and needs seem just as impossible . . . let's remember His Word. When we have 'desert' times in our lives where we feel insecure and lacking, we might question Him as to *how* He will accomplish our requests . . . let's remember His admonition.

"Is the Lord's arm too short?" NO! His powerful, glorious arm is **not too short** to fulfill His Word!

Let us remember: When we are struggling to believe for our miracles, the Lord asks us the question "IS MY ARM TOO SHORT?"

"The fear of the Lord
is the
beginning of wisdom,
and
knowledge of the Holy One
is
understanding."

Proverbs 9:10 (NIV)

LOAD OUR GUN.

"Finally, be strong in the Lord and in his ⅃.
power. Put on the full armor of God so that ⌐ou
can take your stand against the devil's schemes.
For our struggle is not against flesh and blood, but
against the rulers, against the authorities, against
the powers of this dark world and against spiritual
forces of evil in the heavenly realms." Ephesians
6:10-12 (NIV)

We hear much about wars and rumors of wars
and, certainly, this is a time of turbulence
in much of the world. As Christians we have not
been removed from the sounds of war. We are con-
fronted on all sides with fear, doubt, resentment,
discouragement and hopelessness. Our reaction is
to fight and argue with others, only to be discouraged
even more. Paul exhorts us to use the weapons of
God in pulling down the strongholds that wage
war against us. (2 Cor.. 10:4)

*"Wait a minute. This doesn't sound right. What
does it mean 'weapons of God'? I thought a weapon was
what you held in your hand. Also, what is a stronghold
that wages war against us? I thought our problems are
with people. They are the ones we fight. Right?"* It
would appear to be so but, let's examine the

. es in Ephesians more closely.

Most of us understand what 'be strong in the Lord' means. Our spiritual strength comes from God and His power. We are to be strengthened and enabled by Him. If we stopped here, we would be way ahead. Just the knowledge that we need His strength and enabling would keep us out of a lot of trouble.

So many of us react in anger and fear to our adversaries. We have been 'trained' to respond to verbal assaults by, *"I'll let them know what I think of them!" "They will be sorry they did that to me!"* Normally we form this 'training' in our childhoods. Our families and peers were 'training' us when we didn't realize it. Remember the proverb, **"Train** a child in the way he should go, and when he is old he will not turn from it." Proverbs 22:6 (NIV) Unfortunately, many of us were trained in a negative, undesirable way and we definitely need to depart from it.

Paul shows us another way. ". . . be strong **in the Lord,** and in **His** mighty power" Confusing? Not really. Before we came to know Jesus, we had a different lord. *We* were our only defense and answer (if we could find any) to the cares of our lives. It is so very tiring, if not impossible, to have the whole responsibility of our lives. Now we have the LORD and HIS power to protect and direct us. What wonderful news!

"Put on the full armor of God so that you can take your stand against the devil's schemes." The armor referred to in Ephesians is talking about spiritual armament. The illustration conveying that we are to be totally covered by God. The continuing verses in Ephesians describe the believer's armor. The schemes of the devil are the different plans used to deceive, entrap and ruin mankind. We can see the vital importance of God's armor! We can also remember when we experienced a 'scheme' of the devil taking place in our lives.

"For our struggle is not against flesh and blood, but against the rulers, against the authorities, against the powers of this dark world and against the spiritual forces of evil in the heavenly realms." What many of us do not realize is that we struggle against these spiritual entities and not people.

I certainly did not comprehend this life-changing fact when I came to know the Lord. Most of us get angry, hurt and offended by others. If the hurts are by people in our church, often we back away from God. We hear expressions like, *If that is the way Christians treat each other, who needs them!" "They are all **hypocrites!**" "I just won't go back to church!"* (Sounds like a 'scheme' of the devil to me.) Sadly they don't return to church, become even more bitter and fall away from the One who lovingly died for them. "For our struggle is not against flesh and blood. . ."

To further illustrate, let us imagine a man in his home who is under attack by relentless enemies. He has a gun and bullets laying beside him, but he doesn't load the gun. As his fear increases, with his heart racing, he cries out for someone to help him against his attackers. Although he has the earthly weapon to defend himself and his family, he does not use it. We observe his enemies with twisted evil grins

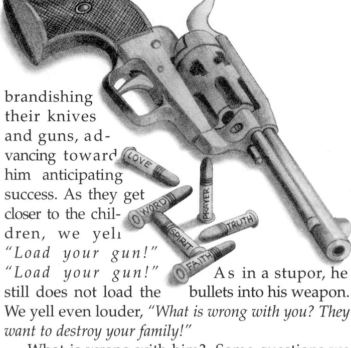

brandishing their knives and guns, advancing toward him anticipating success. As they get closer to the children, we yell *"Load your gun!" "Load your gun!"* As in a stupor, he still does not load the bullets into his weapon. We yell even louder, *"What is wrong with you? They want to destroy your family!"*

What is wrong with him? Some questions we might ask about the man in the illustration: Why doesn't he load his gun? Does he think it won't do any good? Maybe he does not know how to load it? Is he too tired to save himself or his family? Does he feel someone else will save them? Or, maybe he doesn't even know the weapon is beside him.

In like manner, perhaps we need to look at ourselves. When we do not realize we struggle against spiritual entities, we do not 'load our guns' so to speak. We have been instructed to put on the whole armor of God. We have authorities, powers and rulers of darkness with crooked evil grins intent on attacking us and our families. Jesus has given us His word, promises and authority. Why don't we load *our* guns against them? Do we act like the man in this illustration? We need to see if the same questions apply to us.

Our weapons are mighty through the Spirit but they also lay dormant beside us until we 'load' our spirits (guns) with God's words, promises and authority. These spiritual bullets are "mighty through God to the pulling down of strongholds." We do as 2 Corinthians 10:5 admonishes, "Casting down imaginations, and every high thing that exalteth itself against the knowledge of God, and bringing into captivity every thought to the obedience of Christ"; (KJV)

When the 'schemes of the devil' such as fear, doubt, resentment, discouragement and hopelessness attack us, we say, *"NO! I cast down these imaginations and thoughts! I will not feel or react as they are suggesting!"* As we meditate on the words of Christ, we realize our arsenal of spiritual weapons is truly mighty. We no longer have to be afraid of attackers. Our words agree with the Lord and the enemy is defeated in our lives!

Let us remember: We must always LOAD OUR GUNS!

"A happy heart makes the face
cheerful,
but heartache crushes the spirit."

Proverbs 15:13 (NIV)

MENTAL MUSCLES

"For as he thinketh in his heart, so is he: . . ." Proverbs 23:7 (KJV)

"And the second is like unto it. Thou shalt love thy neighbour as thyself." Matthew 22:39 (KJV)

W e all have heard of the benefits and results of exercise. The magazines, newspapers, TV and billboards scream the messages of fitness. The picture perfect men and women modeling the exercise equipment show what we will achieve after only a 'few short months'! We look at them, assess our bodies and determine to try . . . again. Sound familiar?

In our pursuit to improve ourselves, we often forget an equally (if not more) important facet of development found in Proverbs. "As we think in our hearts, so we are." That could be good or, in many cases, bad news.

A highly successful businessman I know is recognized for his motivational speaking about the profound importance of positive reinforcement in our lives and how detrimental negative words are in their impact. He shares that by the time we are twenty-five years of age, 75 percent of all we have been told about ourselves and life has been negative. What a startling realization!

An illustration of that fact is etched in my mind. While my husband and I were eating in a restaurant, we overheard a married couple conversing at the next table. Their young son was trying to enter their conversation with his opinion. His attempts to express himself were met with sighs of annoyance. Finally his father raised his voice very forcefully shouting, *"Shut up, you don't know what you are talking about! You never know anything!"* Their son lowered his head and stopped trying to express his ideas. The negative words went to his heart and were lodged in his self-image. Quite possibly the parents might have wondered why he became so withdrawn.

There can be many more illustrations of negative treatment in our lives. It is hard, if not impossible, to love our neighbors as ourselves when we are so depleted. Since we are so devoid of positive words concerning us, we often try to find worth in 'outside' endeavors. These endeavors can range from our professions to sports or even personal relationships. There are many who must have the latest style in clothing or automobiles to feel acceptable.

When we realize our physical negativity, we know that assertive actions are necessary for change. In like manner, to break out of the negative mental indoctrination, we have to take assertive actions. We can compare the exercises of our thought lives as 'mental muscles' being exercised.

On a daily basis, we need to agree with God's Word concerning our value. Remember, we are **so** important, that Jesus died for us to show our tremendous value. Can anyone think of anything greater? We have to force our mental muscles to think we are beloved with worth, purpose and attractiveness.

Just as physical exercise takes time and repetition, the mental change does not happen with the first exercise. The 'no pain, no gain' rule does not apply with these mental exercises. However, just as our physical muscles react to being altered, the mind will resist the change in thoughts. We are encouraged in Romans 12:2, "Do not **conform** any longer to the pattern of this world, but be **transformed** by the renewing of your mind. Then you will be able to test and approve what God's will is - His good, pleasing and perfect will." (NIV)

When the old 'mental tapes' of negative words play in our minds, STOP THEM! We must insert a new 'mental tape' that says we are valued, attractive, and worthy. Before long, our weak mental muscles will increase and grow with each exercise. Don't give up! You can make it! Being consistent to agree with God's Word on a daily basis is the key. For example, when a thought comes to your mind *"I am unattractive and inferior"*, you reply *"No! Psalms 139:14 says I am fearfully and wonderfully made. That is what I believe. I agree with God and not this thought!"*

The thoughts can be as numerous and varied as our many different personalities and weaknesses. But if they do not agree with what God says we are in Christ Jesus, we must resist them and agree with Him. His promises covers all our problems, hopes and dreams. 1 Timothy 6:12 exhorts us to "Fight the good fight of faith . . . " (NIV) We must use both our bodies and **minds** to God's glory.

Let us remember: We must exercise our MENTAL MUSCLES to God's glory.

MESSY CLOSETS

"The Spirit of the Lord God is upon me; because the Lord hath anointed me to preach good tidings unto the meek; he hath sent me to bind up the brokenhearted, to proclaim liberty to the captives, and the opening of the prison to them that are bound;" Isaiah 61:1 (KJV)

W hat do messy closets have to do with the beloved scripture in Isaiah? Let's find out.

Closets come in all sizes and shapes with varying degrees of neatness. Most of us have had messy closets one time or another. Sometimes the messiness was due to being rushed, not having time to straighten up the jumbled articles. Other times, it was possibly due to an attitude of *"Why bother?" "Who cares?"* or *"Maybe I'll do it tomorrow."*

It is believed that the way we keep our appearances and surroundings is an expression of our mental condition. Depression leads to depressed attitudes about life. While under this affliction, we lose the mental energy to clean up, create and see life with vitality. Some of us have suffered such depression or know someone who is subject to this debilitating, fatiguing condition. One day follows another without goals or the desire to accomplish new things - just getting through the day becomes the only victory. Having the latest hairstyle or clothing seems like too much work and not worth the effort. The zest once experienced about life seems more like a memory.

Depression can come about because of grief or unfulfilled goals in life. Many successful business men and business women, after losing their jobs of many years, sink into swirling pools of depression. So much of their lives were put into the job that has now disappeared. They feel their identities have also disappeared into dark, engulfing holes of anger, hopelessness and fear. The prevailing thoughts are *"What do I do now?" "What can I do now?"* With those who have suffered the loss of loved ones, the same distressing thoughts envelop their minds. So much of their lives were put into the person who has now disappeared.

The outward appearance of a person in a depressed state is easier to recognize. When people who once dressed neatly and fashionably appear in crumpled, unkempt clothes and having a lack of personal hygiene, depression can be suspected. If investigated, the occurrence of tragedy or hardship may be discovered.

Other times those depressed can look clean and orderly, but still have inward, silent turmoil of mental and emotional pain or even unconfessed sin that cannot be seen. These people put on acceptable faces and appearances for others to see, but inside have feelings of loneliness, grief, disappointment and discouragement. This facade can be compared to a house being clean visibly but

having messy closets. The closets are not seen unless investigated. Most of the time people, who are suffering inwardly, do not want others to see their depression, so they work very hard to keep their emotional closet doors closed. When asked how they are feeling, their normal reply will be *"Fine!"*

We all can have messy closets mentally or emotionally. Our inward turmoil can reveal these closets in constant worry or more noticeably in depressing hopelessness. Extreme outbursts of

99

anger or addicting drug and alcohol abuse are not uncommon.

What can we do? The good news is we have the availability of a highly efficient, totally trained cleaning service. His name is Jesus. *This* is what messy closets have to do with the beloved scripture in Isaiah! Jesus came to clean out our messy closets by preaching good tidings to the meek, binding up the brokenhearted, proclaiming liberty to the captives and the opening of the prison (or closets) for them that are bound.

We must let Jesus into our hidden rooms of emotional pain for His life-giving cleaning. He is very careful not to injure our sensitive, hurting hearts. However, He is extremely thorough not to miss the little unthought-of places that need straightening and repair. The hard to reach areas of forgotten, painful memories are efficiently wiped clean by the healing touch of the Holy Spirit. We can trust Him to totally complete His loving cleaning and have a lifetime guarantee of satisfaction and peace. His rates are beyond anything we can pay monetarily - our only charge is to trust and believe in His ability to deliver us. We will find after we let Him clean one closet and feel the peace and joy, we will gladly ask Him to return to clean the remaining closets.

I'll never forget when Jesus entered my hidden emotional closets. Outwardly, I had the appearance of a fun-filled person. I had hidden my messy closets since childhood. Being raised in an alcoholic family brought with it fearful nights of violence and shame-filled poverty. Others did not know about my past since I became adept in concealing it. However, there was One who did know.

As I was praying one night, memories rose in my mind of my childhood. I saw the house I lived in as a child. In each room I experienced different emotional pains. In the bleak kitchen, there was fear and apprehension. This was the room in which my parents would fight (many times violently). The living room contained poverty and shame because our furniture was old and threadbare. My bedroom brought back memories of consuming tears, loneliness and abject despair. What I experienced during this time of remembering began a major healing in my life I did not realize I needed.

As I visualized these 'tucked away' memories and experienced the forgotten emotions, Jesus appeared in the midst of my memory. He took me by the hand and walked with me to each room. We began in the dreaded kitchen. I saw my parents fighting with long knives in their hands, and the paralyzing fear I experienced as a child rushed over me again. Jesus then stepped between them, His extended arms blocking my view. Great, unexplained peace descended upon me. My heart stopped beating wildly, and the gnawing fear I had lived with for so long seemed to melt away.

He then took me to the living room. Once again the feelings of shame over that room enveloped me. As I was feeling so ashamed of our poverty, He took His right arm and with a large sweeping motion transformed the room. Everything became sparkling clean and new! When His arm swept the room, the shame and

101

poverty were wiped clean from my heart.

I continued to follow Him as He walked into my bedroom. This was a room I never wanted to remember again. I saw the sagging bed by the window and the old brown dresser. My eyes also went to the dark closet where I had cried countless tears. Again I experienced the persistent tears and dark despair I had hidden so deeply within me. He lifted His wonderful, strong arm and swept the darkened room changing it into a room of brightness and sunshine!

Standing very still, I realized a brand new, wonderful feeling was permeating my whole being. I felt peace I had not felt before. I knew I was healed. Jesus had bound up my broken heart and healed my emotional messy closets. Then, He disappeared.

I realized later I had experienced what Isaiah described in the sixty-first chapter. Since that night, I have asked Jesus to heal other plaguing memories and continue to do so as others arise. His arms are just as strong now as they were then.

When any of us find a wonderful, caring cleaning service, we will tell others - as I have told you. You, in turn, can tell those you know, so they can have their closet doors opened to receive His miraculous inward healing.

Let us remember: Jesus died to clean out the MESSY CLOSETS of our hearts!

"MY CHILD DON'T EVER STOP LOVING ME"

"But Peter declared, 'Even if I have to die with you, I will never disown you.' And all the other disciples said the same." Matthew 26:35 (NIV)

Many of us have felt the zealousness of Peter. We feel the deep love of commitment for the Lord and could join Peter's chorus of commitment. *"Even if I have to die with you, I will never disown you."* However, the scriptures reveal that strong, faithful Peter did deny Jesus - although he would never have considered the possibility. After all, he felt he was too strong! He had too much love for his Lord! Right? I understand. I've been there. I did not deny Jesus, but I did drift away from Him. What I thought was unthinkable happened to me.

It's been a few years now, but it is still etched in my mind. After a series of emotionally draining trials, some of which resulted in anger and bitterness towards other people, I backed away from God. Sound familiar? Many of us have been 'Peters' and have not realized it. When we are offended, normally the first thing we do is stop fellowshipping with other believers. Then over

103

time, we find our relationship with God is 'not quite the same'. Something is wrong but we can't quite put our finger on it. We just know, *"If that's the way Christians act, we don't want to be around them!"* A root of bitterness forms and smothers our tender relationship with the God we loved so ardently. But, Jesus is the same loving, forgiving God for us as He was for Peter. He lovingly accepts us when we return to Him. Perhaps you can relate to the story I am about to share.

After an extended period of praise and worship to the Lord, He spoke to me in my heart, *"My child don't ever stop loving me."* I immediately said, *"Oh no, Lord that will never happen!"* I was perplexed about why He spoke those words to me, but felt confident of my relationship of love for Him.

Not long after the Lord spoke to me, I was enjoying my little two-year old daughter with her sparkling blue eyes and curly red hair. We were both on her bed laughing and holding on to each other seeing who could hug each other the tightest. Without thinking, I held her close and said, *"Dawne, don't ever stop loving me."* Her love felt so good! I didn't want it to ever end.

Then I remembered the Lord's words to me. I

felt I understood. I was enjoying her company so much and feeling the love in our hearts toward each other, I wanted that moment to last forever. But, I also knew that as she grew to be a young woman there would be times she wouldn't understand why she would have to go against her will and obey. Also, there would be times when she would not appear to love me as much because of the changes in her life. I didn't want that! Couldn't she stay my loving two-year old forever? No, both she and I had to grow.

Over the years, she and I did have our times of strained relationships and changes. There were moments when I wondered if the stresses and strains had affected our love. But, through all the tense and trying times, our underlying love remained, and even grew deeper and richer.

Through the years, in my relationship with Jesus, there have been times of my wondering why I had to change and do what He said in His Word. It also did not appear that I loved Him as much as I once expressed to him. Why couldn't I remain spiritually, the loving two-year old? I have to grow!

If I had my choice, I would stay a spiritual two-year old forever. If given a choice, perhaps Dawne would have remained two years old enjoying her dolls and her child world. But we both had to grow, Dawne physically and I spiritually. Through the tense and trying times spiritually, my underlying love for the Lord did remain, even growing deeper and richer.

Just as Peter was so sure of his level of total

commitment to Jesus but failed to remain, we all may have our moments of strained relationships with our Lord. We are the tense ones and He is always calm. Peter, under intense pressure, denied Him. Unfortunately, when we have our 'intense pressures', we also might back away from Him.

What do we do? We do as Peter. We ask forgiveness and return to Jesus. He forgave Peter and the other disciples, encouraging them to continue in their walk of faith with Him.

We all go through our years of spiritual development with the turbulent times of doubt and uncertainty. But, during these events, if we stray, we must also receive Jesus' forgiveness and continue *our* walk of faith with Him. He still lovingly says, *"My child don't ever stop loving me ."*

Let us remember: Jesus is saying to us, "MY CHILD DON'T EVER STOP LOVING ME."

NOT HOW BUT WHO

"But seek first his kingdom and his righteousness, and all these things will be given to you as well."
Matthew 6:33 (NIV)

"And my God will meet all your needs according to his glorious riches in Christ Jesus."
Philippians 4:19 (NIV)

"*H*ow *are you going to do it?*" "**When** *will you do it?*"

We sigh and tell our children for what seems to be the hundredth time, *"I will do it!" "I don't know exactly how, but it will be done!" "You just have to trust me!"* This answer works for a while but, when they still don't see their request evidenced soon enough for them, they entreat again. *"Oh, please, please, please do it!"* This continual lack of trust starts to hurt us and sometimes with exasperation we burst out saying, *"Trust me!" "I know what I'm doing!" "Won't you just **trust me?**"* Sound familiar?

The inability to trust usually forms in childhood. Many times our parents weren't perfect in accomplishing all we felt we needed and a lack of faith in their performance developed. We could only see them through a child's eyes of dependence. We weren't able to see the daily trials and problems that exist in the life of an adult. So, when they weren't fulfilling our requests soon enough, we doubted.

We grow up to be adults and read, "And my God will meet all your needs . . . " We think to ourselves, *"This is such a nice, easy scripture to read from my 'daily promises' box. I sure do love knowing He will meet all my needs."* Tucking it into our memories with the other scriptures of daily promises, we feel secure.

All goes well for a while; however, the day comes when we have a need we can't supply. Our dialog within ourselves begins. *"**Oh no**! What am I going to do? Where is that scripture? It says something about God doing things for me. Where is it? Oh yes, here it is."* *'And my God will meet all your needs according to his glorious riches in Christ Jesus.'* *"I **have** to pray about this one because **I sure can't do it**. It has to be a miracle. Why does this have to happen to me?"* (Gulp) Here goes . . . *"Uh, God, I ask for _____ to happen in my life. You say you'll provide all my needs and this is definitely a need! Thank you for doing this for me. Amen."*

Our dialog continues, *"I hope He answers me. I need to know right away! I don't see how it can be done. I wonder **how** He will do it? I wonder **when** He will do it! Oh God please, please, please do it!"* Does this dialog also sound familiar?

Aren't we glad our parent God is patient with our questions of doubt. Learning to trust Him is a growing process. Just as we saw our natural parents from a child's eyes, we view our majestic Father the same way. It is an entirely different world for us to enter a dependency on God. We are so used to running our own lives. It is very difficult to 'let go' and believe in someone else.

We are given an entire Bible with scriptures that assure us of God supplying our needs and desires. When we want to apply them, our thoughts trip us up with the one big question we have asked since childhood. HOW? How *can* He do it? How *will* He do it? How is it possible? Since we can't imagine how God will supply, we doubt.

But, here might be a key to help us. It is not **'how'** our prayers will be answered, but **'Who'** will answer! We can find out just Who will answer our prayers by reading and believing His book of instructions and promises. He will patiently reveal Himself to us and show us the ways to believe in Him. But, we must do our part. Romans 10:17 tells us, "So then faith cometh by hearing, and hearing by the word of God." (KJV) We are to read, listen and meditate on the Word of God daily and faith comes! Our part is to believe, His part is to answer!

Let us remember: It is NOT HOW BUT WHO. Our part is to believe, His part is to answer.

"The eyes of the Lord
are everywhere,
keeping watch on the wicked
and the good."

Proverbs 15:3 (NIV)

OUR RESPONSIBILITY
IS TO RECEIVE

"And when he sees all that is accomplished by the anguish of his soul, he shall be satisfied; . . ."
Isaiah 53:11 (TLB)

Responsibility!
We have heard this word most of our lives. While growing up, many of us were told, *"Behave like a responsible person."* If we did something wrong, *"You didn't act very responsibly."* When we are older we are admonished, *"You are a responsible adult now. Act like one!"*

Showing ourselves responsible has always been a high priority. But, there is more than one way to look at this valuable quality. The Funk and Wagnalls Standard Desk Dictionary's definition of responsibility is, "The state of being responsible or accountable. That for which one is answerable; a duty or trust." With this definition in mind, let's look at 'responsibility' in a way we perhaps have not realized, but an area that is of the utmost importance.

Since we accepted Jesus as our Lord, we have read or been told of His great and wonderful sacrifices for us. With this knowledge, we are presented with two very important questions. When we read about the cruel, demonic inspired beating Jesus received before the Cross showing the depth of His love for us, what are we to do with this heart-rending occurrence? When we remember His painful, life-sacrificing crucifixion along with His life-changing words, *"It is finished!"*, what are we to do with

this memory? Interesting questions that need to have answers.

We must, indeed, forever remember these love-filled, sacrificial acts; but along with remembering, we have a responsibility. *"Responsibility? How can I be responsible for something that happened over two thousand years ago? I know I have the responsibility to live a good life and treat others with kindness and love." "Is there more?"*

Yes, and that is what we will look into further. Responsibility can be more than good acts of conduct. It can also involve *'receiving'*. *"Receiving? I thought to be responsible only meant giving and doing!"* Yes, we are to give and do for others as God commanded. However, there is also more.

It is our responsibility to *receive all* of the victory and freedom that Jesus died to give us! We are to *receive all* of His faithful Word and His life-giving promises. This is our part, but we can be much too complacent and take our responsibility lightly. If we do not *receive all* that He provided for us before, during and after the Cross, His sacrifice is not fully utilized. Although eternal life and forgiveness of our sins reach beyond our ability for which we can express thanksgiving and praise, there is more. The rest are still waiting. The abundant life, health, prosperity and peace are also ours.

Why don't we do it? Why don't we apply and receive all? Reasons can vary from lack of knowledge, wrong teaching, feeling of unworthiness, disappointment in God, etc., but, the promises still lay there. It is usually our tendency as children of the Lord to ask, ask, ask. As our relationship grows with Jesus, we start to think about what *we* can do for Him and not so much of what *He* can do for us.

Although we will always gratefully ask Him for our needs and desires, there is something we can do *for* Him. We can give Him heartfelt praise and *receive all* that He provided before, during and after the Cross. Not receiving all that He did can mean we are not fully accepting His loving, life-giving sacrifice for us. As we receive, **we show forth His giving!**

Our 'receiving' is different when we receive all of His provisions because of the motivation to *please* Him. Because we love Him, we receive His indescribable love and all-consuming sacrifice to give us a free and victorious life. "And when he sees all that is accomplished by the anguish of his soul, he shall be satisfied; . . ."

"Now I understand . . . we do have a responsibility!"

Let us remember: OUR RESPONSIBILITY IS TO RECEIVE.

RING AND SANDALS

"I will set out and go back to my father and say to him: Father, I have sinned against heaven and against you. I am no longer worthy to be called your son; make me like one of your hired men. So he got up and went to his father.

"But while he was still a long way off, his father saw him and was filled with compassion for him; he ran to his son, threw his arms around him and kissed him.

"The son said to him, 'Father, I have sinned against heaven and against you. I am no longer worthy to be called your son.'

"But the father said to his servants, 'Quick!' Bring the best robe and put it on him. Put a ring on his finger and sandals on his feet. Bring the fattened calf and kill it. Let's have a feast and celebrate. For this son of mine was dead and is alive again; he was lost and is found.' So they began to celebrate." Luke 15: 18-24 (NIV)

T hese inspiring, grace-filled scriptures in Luke are referred to as the story of the 'prodigal son'. This beloved parable is one with which most of us are acquainted. However, we must remember it was told years ago to a group of people that lived differently than we do today.

If one of our children returned home after being presumed dead; we would, of course, be overjoyed beyond description! After hugging them for hours, we would probably joyfully prepare a meal in celebration. Our story would be the same as the one in Luke, except we would not think to give our returned child a ring and sandals. Since we do not have these customs, we might not see a

deep
truth of
this parable.

The sandals and ring were very significant to the people during the time of Luke. These two items were worn by people showing pride and dignity. The slaves' shoes were many times taken from them so they wouldn't run away. Although the times and customs were different, some things remain the same. We still have our prodigal sons and daughters today.

In the parable, when the prodigal son left his father's home, he thought he was entering freedom. How many of our children have said, "*I want to be free! I'm tired of these stupid rules!"* (We all know what the trap of 'being free' and the lack of rules does to young people.)

The prodigal in Luke ended up being stripped of his freedom along with his respect and self-worth. Furthering his disgrace, he resorted to tending pigs which was considered the most degrading job for that time and culture. When his hunger became so extreme, he even wanted the food of the pigs but was not allowed.

This could be a story of many runaway sons and daughters today. We hear the tragedies of their lives 'on the street'. Their once-prized freedom ends in the degrading captivity of poverty and sin. Many tell of being hungry for days and foraging through garbage cans for 'prizes' of stale bread or rancid meat. The petty complaints about their food at home are forgotten in their frantic quest for survival.

Upon returning home in this condition of bondage and degradation, the prodigal admitted his sin and unworthiness to his father. Though he might have expected to be beaten or rebuked for his rebellion, his return home brought exceeding joy to both him and his father.

Seeing his son, the father excitedly ran to him and kissed him. With much love, he showed his wayward prodigal the state he had entered by returning home: a state of grace. His son's pride and dignity were restored with honor, signified with the gift of the ring and sandals. The father greatly rejoiced, for his son once lost, was found!

Today we may feel to go the way of the world

is to have freedom. But it becomes painfully apparent that our rebellious delusion only ends in unthinkable captivity. The world's way of living has a glitter to it that only disguises the fence rails of the pig pen! Just as the prodigal son in Luke, our only hope is to return to our loving Father ... He is waiting with our ring and sandals.

Let us remember: When we return home, our RING AND SANDALS will be waiting.

SYMPTOMS

"All wrongdoing is sin: . . ." 1 John 5:17 (NIV)

"*War in Bosnia! More details later after the following announcements.*"

"*The 'First Savings Bank' on North Main was **robbed** today by two armed men. They were apprehended and are in jail awaiting trial.*"

"*The President of Township Research Corporation* was found dead in his affluent home in the Southeast section of town. A **murder** investigation is in progress!*"

"*Two **abused** children were discovered in a closet of their home. They apparently had not eaten for three days! Their parents were away for the weekend.*"

"*A **pornography** ring was raided today by police officers! The proprietors of the business left before being arrested and are still being pursued by law enforcement officials.*"

Click! Off goes the 11:00 news. We sigh and go to bed another night with these 'good news' reports on our hearts and minds. We think to ourselves, "*What can I do about all these horrible things? There is so much bad news! I wish it were different but, there isn't anyway one person can make a difference! There is just too much!*" *Right?*"

Let's see if there is something we can do. There are many tragic occurrences in the world: wars, crimes, divorce, child abuse, pornography, drugs, etc. We see them as individual problems with individual solutions.

Since crime is on the increase, law enforcement has declared 'war' on crime! Child abuse and pornography are epidemic, so more agencies are

created because of this savagery. Divorces are rampant, which results in more counseling centers for these unfortunate people.

All these agencies are good and well-intended. However, if we look at these tragedies more closely, we see a common thread. In each case, there is a lack of one thing and an abundance of another.

The scripture states in Matthew 7:20, " Thus, by their fruit you will recognize them." (NIV) *"Fruit? What do you mean? I thought we were talking about crime, drugs etc. When I think of fruit, I think of something I eat!"*

Yes, we all know fruit such as apples and oranges are to be eaten. However, the fruit mentioned in Matthew is a condition of a person's spirit. One definition of fruit in the Funk and Wagnalls Standard Desk Dictionary is, "The outcome, consequence or result of some action, effort."

The fruit of the Spirit is described in the fifth chapter of Galatians, as having the attributes of love, joy, peace,patience, kindness, goodness, faithfulness,gentleness and self-control . . . Whereas, the works of the sinful nature contain sexual immorality, impurity, debauchery, idolatry and witchcraft, hatred, discord jealousy, fits of rage, selfish ambition, dissensions, factions and envy; drunkenness, orgies, and the like. Are joy and goodness found in the tragedy of life? Or, is there found just the opposite; an abundance of hate, self-centerness and greed.

*"O.K. I understand there is good and evil 'fruit' in the world. How did it get here? Has it always been around? **And, what can I do about it!"***

The attributes of the sinful nature described above, are the results of **sin**! 1 John 5:17 clearly tells us, "All wrongdoing is sin." Sin was the opposite of God when it came into the world. God is **love** in all of it's meanings.

Sin shows itself in the confusion of humankind. A divorce is not just a relationship breakdown between two people; it is a relationship breakdown with God by either one or both parties. Crime is not just an assault against society. It is an assault by Satan against humankind. Wars, child abuse and social wrongdoing are all symptoms. These destructive symptoms are the opposite of God . . . symptoms of sin.

"But, what can I do?"

Since we know the tragedies of society are the result of sins, we can have a vital participation! First, if we are part of the cause, we do our part by aligning ourselves with God and break away from Satan's grasp. Jesus came to enable us to walk the victorious life.

Next, we can **PRAY!** When we hear the bad news on TV or radio blaring life's tragedies, let's don't just agree with its evil, but pray for hearts to change right away!

We do have something we can do. Symptoms can be changed. Our hope is in God! We can begin with ourselves and pray for others!

Let us remember: When we see SYMPTOMS of sin, recognize its true source and pray!

* Fictional name

THE SPIRIT OF XMAS

"But what about you?" he asked. "Who do you say I am?" Simon Peter answered, "You are the Christ, the Son of the Living God." Matthew 16:15,16 (NIV)

What do you feel when you hear the words, *"It's only one month to Christmas!"* Many people that I hear speak these words with almost a feeling of dread.

What do we envision Christmas to be? The image of people rushing around buying presents, baking continually and general fatigue comes to many minds. It is almost a relief when December 26th arrives! How sad. The true meaning of Christmas often is swallowed up in the whirlpool of busyness, spending and debt. Let us take a moment to reflect on this wonderful day right now.

We hear and read the phrase "Merry Xmas." The early Christians substituted the word "Christ" with an 'X' to protect themselves from persecution. Today, however, since most of us do not fear persecution for our beliefs, deleting 'Christ' in Christmas has been done either deliberately or in ignorance. Putting an 'X' may seem a trendy thing to say or write but, in reality, including the name of 'Christ' is of the highest importance! The word 'Christ' which is concerning Jesus, the Savior of the world, means "Anointed One."

Man refers to the exciting time of the year in December as "Christmas." Taking out the 'Christ' and inserting an 'X' is for him to delete the reason for celebration. Jesus was born and anointed to redeem, heal, deliver and bring salvation to all people - to us! What wonderful news!

There is a total contrast between the spirit of Xmas and spirit of Christmas. The spirit of Xmas involves rushing, fatigue and debt. The spirit of **Christ**mas is one of giving, peace and love. If we take 'Christ' out of Christmas, it results in just a day of exhausting activities.

Just as He asked His disciples who did *they* think He was, He also asks us who do *we* think He is. Do we insert an 'X' in our Christmas? As Peter responded in Matthew, we must know Jesus to be the *Christ* ("Anointed One"), the Son of the living God, for our lives every day!

When we know Him to be our "Anointed One," we must resist behaving in a spirit of Xmas. Let's make this Christmas a true celebration of His birthday!

Let us remember: Keep THE SPIRIT OF XMAS out of our **Christ**mas!

124

THE WALLS CAME TUMBLING DOWN

"Therefore everyone who hears these words of mine and puts them into practice is like a *wise man* who built his house on the rock. The rain came down, the streams rose, and the winds blew and beat against that house; yet it did not fall, because it had its foundation on the rock. But everyone who hears these words of mine and does not put them into practice is like a foolish man who built his house on sand. The rain came down, the streams rose, and the winds blew and beat against that house, and it fell with a great crash." Matthew 7:24-27 (NIV)

"*He has so much wisdom!*"
It is a fine compliment to be called a person with wisdom. We feel good about ourselves when others comment, *"That was a wise decision you made!" "You sure are wise."* or *"You have wisdom beyond your years!"* Those words go deep into our hearts.

We strive to be prudent in our decisions in life. We buy enough life insurance, set aside savings for our children's college educations, establish investment accounts, save for emergencies and plan for retirement. Whew! We've got everything covered. Right? But, there is more. Let's look closer.

The scriptures in Matthew tell of another form of wisdom and, conversely, being foolish. Jesus stated, "Therefore everyone who hears these words of mine and puts them into practice is like a *wise man*, . . . " What wonderful words said about us from the great God of creation! Those words go deep into our hearts. Right?. . . or do they?

We first have to *hear* and then *do* what He says. But, this is the greatest wisdom of all. What we do with Jesus' sayings will not only equip us in our lives now, but for eternity. Let's look further into these exhorting scriptures.

It is noteworthy that both individuals, the wise and the foolish man, built houses and stormy

conditions came to pass. Building our lives can be equated with the construction of houses. A house must have the proper foundation to support it, with much attention given to insure safety and longevity. We all have seen homes that have been destroyed by storms, while others weather the same storms and stand firm. Proper supports and strong foundations were most likely missing from the demolished houses. Unfortunately, in these tragedies, the occupants lose possessions and family treasures. In worst cases, they may even lose their loved ones with the many "if onlys" on their lips. What loss, what grief!

When a weak area is discovered in the foundation of a house, we know a good amount of time and expense must be expended to correct the problem. However, if a house has a proper foundation, it can withstand storms of varying intensity. We can see the comparison of the foundations of a house to our lives and marriages.

Let's look at a scenario. On a warm Sunday afternoon, after a satisfying midday meal, we decide to take a pleasant walk through our neighborhood. As we walk along enjoying the fragrant flowers and vivid shrubbery, we notice the Jones' house leaning precariously to the side. It startles us and leaves us wondering what has happened! It didn't look that way before! We decide we will ask them about it later and continue our walk.

Much to our surprise, the next ten houses are leaning or have totally fallen down! Now we are really alarmed! *"What in the world is going on?"* *"Are there problems in the ground?" "Has there been a massive termite infestation?" "Are their foundations sinking?"* We are really troubled! Our anxiety continues, *"Will it happen to us?" "Are we safe?" "What should we do?"* There, obviously, is a reason for great concern. This requires immediate attention!

This fictitious disaster is most assuredly alarming. However, there is another destructive epidemic occurring all around us; *the destruction of lives and marriages.* Each life or marriage leaning to the side or totally collapsed has a foundational problem.

Unfortunately, we have grown accustomed to this ruin. When we become aware of another statistic of devastation in a life, often we do not give it a great deal of thought. The abundance of emotional and physical disorders have desensitized our ability to be a caring and responsive people.

The scriptures admonish us that if God is not 'the rock' in our lives, we will not have the proper foundation to support the trials and stresses of life. The *wise man* knew a rock foundation was the answer for weathering storms. Jesus indicated that hearing and doing His Word becomes our life's rock.

The foolish man may hear also; but by not following through on the Lord's instructions, his life foundation is only able to support him during the easy times. The storms come and it is discovered very quickly and decidedly that the support is not sufficient. His life falls with great impact!

Do you know those whose lives are on sandy ground? They appear fine under good conditions but when a storm breaks upon them, they fall apart. Do you know those whose lives are solid? They appear fine under good and bad conditions. Their foundational rock is the Lord.

We need to make a decision. *"Do I want to be a wise person?"* We have been given the blueprints for our lives. It is a matter of hearing and doing what the contractor of the universe says to do! He is very knowledgeable about building lives. He takes loving care to watch over every detail. Caring so much for the final product, He gave His life to insure its completion. He loves His work. We can be assured everything is handled with absolute quality because He said, *"It is finished."* It really is an offer we can't refuse!

Just as we would not accept homes built on poor foundations, let us not accept the weak areas and construction problems in our lives and marriages. Let's take a walk around our spiritual house and check our foundations. Are there cracks? Has there been an infestation of troubles, fears and hardships? Are our lives safe on a rock rather than on a sand foundation?

Let's decide to go with the 'master builder'. He is the carpenter of our souls. We will feel so good about ourselves when the Lord says, *"That's a wise decision you made! "You have become a **wise person!"***

Let us remember: IF THE WALLS CAME TUMBLING DOWN, examine the foundation!

"A gossip betrays a confidence;
so avoid a man who talks
too much."

Proverbs 20:19 (NIV)

WALK IN LOVE

"A new command I give you: Love one another. As I have loved you, so you must love one another." John 13:34 (NIV)

"My command is this: Love each other as I have loved you." John 15:12 (NIV)

"Be devoted to one another in brotherly love. Honor one another above yourselves." Romans 12:10 (NIV)

"*D*id *you hear what the Pastor said in Church today?" I don't agree with him and it makes me so upset!"*

"Clair Seigrass'* skirt was too short again! She shouldn't look that way in church!"

"Bob Funkly* sang too loud again in the choir as usual!"

"Oh well, see you next Sunday. Have a good week!"

We get into our cars and drive to the nearest restaurant still rehearsing the 'wrongs' of the people in the Sunday morning service. If we see someone we know in the restaurant, we also tell them to see if they agree. We haven't done anything wrong in

DO YOURSELF A FAVOR

relaying these 'facts'. They are the 'truth' and we haven't hurt anybody. Right? Perhaps we have. Let's look closer.

"My command is this: Love each other as I have loved you." *"Oh! But, I didn't do anything really bad by talking about the others in Church today. It was an innocent thing to do and everybody does it. I would never dream of really hurting anybody. They will*

never find out I said those things. So, who does it hurt?"

We read the scriptures that tell us to love one another as Christ loves us. We readily agree with this wonderful message and feel we should strive to accomplish it. If someone asked us the question, *"Do you act as Jesus commanded?"* Our answer might be, *"Yes. Of course there are times when I don't, but I always have a good reason!"* Our love - or lack of it - can manifest itself in different ways.

Let's consider the most important reason we should show love to others. Jesus! He is the head of the body, the church, and each member is a part of *Him.* (Eph. 1:22,23) He declares in Matthew 25:40, "I tell you the truth, whatever you did for

132

one of the least of these brothers of mine, you did for me."

"I never thought of that before!" Many of us haven't. With this realization, our attitudes about those in the body of Christ take on a deeper significance.

As the earlier fictitious conversation relates, we have, at times, spoken negatively about His children. Sometimes our remarks were spoken in innocence or brashly purposeful. One evening, during a meal, my husband and I were duly impressed when a woman told us about her wonderful relationship with Jesus. However, our enthusiasm melted when she continued to relay how she couldn't stand His kids! We would not dream of talking negatively about Jesus or try to bring out His faults or weaknesses. But, many times, we don't hesitate to tell of others shortcomings with vivid descriptions.

"A new *command* I give you: Love one another. As I have loved you, so you must love one another." When we speak negatively of others in His body the Church; we are, in effect, speaking of Jesus. And, conversely, if we speak positively about others, we edify Him! We don't realize when we discuss the weaknesses or faults of those in the Church, we are talking about God's children.

When someone speaks against our children, we take it personally. Our children are an extension of us and we want them to be treated well by others. The question to ask ourselves is, "Whose spiritual child are they?" If we don't know, we should treat them with respect as we should *all* people.

"Be devoted to one another in brotherly love.

Honor one another above yourselves." We know from the scriptures how important His church is to Him - even to the point of His death. He has **commanded** that we love His children as we love Him.

Perhaps, this is an area where we can improve. Let's increase our love for Jesus and out of our overflow extend love to others! We can offer love to Him with words of praise, encouragement, and blessings to and about His children.

"I understand now. I never realized that my words about others can be an offering of love to Him. I definitely want to bless Him and others!"

Let us remember: To WALK IN LOVE with His children is to give an offering of love to Him.

* Fictional names

WINGS!

"He will cover you with his feathers, and under His wings you will find refuge; his faithfulness will be your shield and rampart." Psalms 91:4 (NIV)

I love birds!
They are a wonderful, enjoyable creation of God. We have had several feathered couples over the years build their homes in our various trees. Watching them patiently place straw and twigs together to form just the perfect nesting environ-ment for their upcoming offspring, we applaud their success!

One spring, a diligent couple decided to nest outside our bedroom window. The children were delighted to have them so close. We placed a lad-der close enough to observe the mother bird sit-ting on her nest full of treasures. She would not move although she was aware of our presence.

Awakening one morning, we heard additional excited 'cheeps'. Looking outside, we realized her patient, dutiful efforts were rewarded by four active, healthy and very hungry newborns! They became our family project to photograph their day-to-day development. It was a joy to hear the faint 'chirps' as they waited for 'Mom and Dad' to return with their meals of delicious worms and bugs.

The babies developed nicely and before long totally outgrew their small nest. We realized the fateful day had come to leave their safe, protected environment. Oh no! We knew what dangers awaited them!

Our neighborhood is a cat lovers haven. We have short hair and long hair felines of all descriptions and dubious origins. These inquisitive, adept hunters make our backyard a regular stop on their daily prowls throughout the neighborhood.

When those little, helpless birds flopped out of their nest on to the ground, we became the tiny creatures' guardians. We often chased away the 'evil' cats licking their mouths in anticipation of a delicious snack! After all, they were *our* baby birds! *We* were there when they were born! *We* watched them grow! *We* had to protect them and give them a chance to live! Right? Together with their parents, our vigil was successful for they did live and possibly returned to build their own nests.

There is a striking parallel to my true story and God's love and concern for us. "He will cover you with his feathers, and under his wings you will find refuge; . . ." In many ways we are *His* 'baby birds.' *He* was there when we were born again into His family! *He* watches us grow! *He* knows we must be protected and given a chance to live abundant lives!

Perhaps we can learn something about dependency from the wildlife kingdom. It is so easy to leave the protection of God's wings. When a prayer isn't answered soon enough, we begin to plan how *we* might bring about a satisfactory solution. With this resolve, we slowly leave His loving covering. Or, perhaps it is our tendency to take matters into our own hands and never even enter the safety under His wings.

These examples can be compared to the little ones in their nest. They could decide, *"Mom and Dad are not keeping us warm enough or feeding us as much as we want, so we think we will try it on our own."* They don't realize they aren't developed enough and the hungry cats are circling below. No, birds don't do that. They seem to have more wisdom sometimes than we higher creations of God!

To be covered with His feathers and under His wings is to become as a child that trusts his Father with his life. Yet, how can we become children when we are grown? Jesus said in Matthew 18:3 " . . . unless you change and become like *little children*, you will never enter the kingdom of heaven." (NIV) Children are totally dependent on their parents for their shelter, food and even love. By entrusting our entire being together with our hopes, dreams and plans into His hands and releasing them to Him, we have that same dependency.

This dependent lifestyle is often a difficult area of spiritual development. We are used to controlling our lives. *"I'm afraid to release control!"* *"What if God doesn't come through for me?"* These are understandable fears, but we all must make this life-changing decision. In releasing our control, we will be kept under His loving, protective wings. We stay covered with His feathers and are warmed with His protection of love.

If we have trouble making that decision, remember the wildlife kingdom. After all, we are His 'baby birds'!

Let us remember: We must stay under the covering of His loving, protective WINGS!

"YOU'LL HAVE TO SPEAK UP, *SHE'S* HARD OF HEARING!"

"And why do you look at the speck in your brother's eye, but do not notice the log that is in your own eye?" Matthew 7:3 (NASB)

M y family recounts with amusement the time my husband's aging aunt and uncle visited our home. Many years had passed since their last visit and we looked forward to seeing them. Within a short time of talking and catching up on old times, it became quite apparent that both Aunt and Uncle were extremely hearing impaired. We raised our voices, hoping to compensate for their hearing loss, even to the point of shouting.

After a time of this exerted effort, our voices became hoarse, but we continued trying to talk, not making it apparent we were aware of their deficiency. While we were 'conversing' with my husband's aunt, his uncle loudly interrupted us by yelling *"You'll have to speak up, **she's** hard of hearing!"* His outburst totally surprised us. It took all we had to not burst out laughing since he was as hard of hearing as she was! It was so obvious he did not

139

know the extent of *his* impairment.

This incident, although very amusing at the time, can be seen as a serious illustration to all of us. Too often we judge, criticize or make jokes about people without realizing the weaknesses and faults in our own lives. The Lord admonished, "Do not judge lest you be judged yourselves." (Matt. 7:1) Since others often conduct their lives differently from us, we see their actions as more in error than our own. We unwittingly place ourselves above them as smarter or somehow better. The 'specks' in their eyes look more like huge logs and the 'logs' in our eyes look more like tiny specks.

Jesus proclaimed "And why do you look at the speck in your brother's eye, but do not notice the log that is in your own eye?" A speck is defined as 'a small bit or particle' whereas a log is the dramatic size of a tree trunk. We do not realize the logs in our own eyes blind us

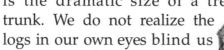

from seeing others clearly. Because of this, we can often miss the wonderful qualities that they may possess. If we judge or criticize, these actions are a clear indication of log size beams in our eyes and our major need for the Lord's forgiveness!

Let us remember: When we are tempted to judge others, we should recall the words "YOU'LL HAVE TO SPEAK UP, *SHE'S* HARD OF HEARING!"

Closing. . .

Thank you for selecting "DO YOURSELF A FAVOR" I trust the thirty-one chapters have given you thirty-one "favors".

I find this book is a "favor" for me since I refer back to it for my own comfort, edification and encouragement. I almost feel removed from being the author and become the reader with my own needs.

When I need more assurance to believe for a financial need, I re-read "Chocolate Covered Cherries" and "Is My Arm Too Short?" When it seems my prayer is taking "forever" to be answered, I re-read, "Not How, But Who", "In Due Season", "A Loyal Friend" and "Draw the Line." I remember and feel encouraged. When I listen to TV news telling of crimes, floods, tornadoes or hear an ambulance wailing in the distance, I remember "Symptoms" and pray. I feel at that moment I somehow make a difference in the lives of unseen faces and their troubles. I am not just a busy person racing through life with my own set of family, friends and challenges.

Thank you, Lord, for giving me this opportunity to write these chapters for all of us. Your Word is our ultimate answer to everything!

May God bless you as you re-read the chapters during your day by day journey in life.

With love,

Frieda

"Let us hold fast the confession of our hope without wavering, for He who promised is faithful; and let us consider how to stimulate one another to love and good deeds, not forsaking our own assembling together, as is the habit of some, but *ENCOURAGING one another;* and all the more, as you see the day drawing near. " Heb. 10:23-25 (NASB)

****

Do you have an ENCOURAGING story to share with others about how God answered prayer, blessed you or revealed His love to you or someone you know?

If you do and would like to pass on this encouragement with others, please print or type it and send to:

NEW VENTURE
P.O. Box 26493,
Greenville, SC 29616

When your treasured story is selected, it will be put in the book "God's Favors"©. You will be notified and your name along with the name of the person for whom it is written (if applicable) will be acknowledged for your submission.

142

Give the gift of
A Favor
to your friends, acquaintances and loved ones.

For additional copies check with your local bookstore or order by sending your check or money order payable to:

NEW VENTURE

P.O. Box 26493 • Greenville, SC 29616 • (864) 292-9095
FAX: (864) 292-9095

I would like ____ copies of "DO YOURSELF A FAVOR" for only $14.95 each, plus $3.00 shipping. (SC residents please add 75¢ state sales tax per book). Canadian orders must have a U.S. funds postal money order.

Shipping:
$3.00 for the first book and $2.00 for each additional book. Allow 3 to 4 weeks for delivery.

My check or money order for $_____ is enclosed.

Print Name: _____

Address: _____

City: _____

State: _____ Zip: _____

Phone: (____) _____

Look forward to the "Favors To Myself Day By Day"calendar, "Favors to Myself Moment by Moment" notepads and audio of the book "DO YOURSELF A FAVOR" to be released in 1999!

LET US REMEMBER

- **A LOYAL FRIEND** is a prized possession!
- When you trust in God's faithfulness, you can **BELIEVE FOR YOUR DREAM.**
- No request is too small, not even **CHOCOLATE-COVERED CHERRIES!**
- We should not speak **CORRUPT COMMUNICATIONS** but rather attractive words of grace to the hearers.
- "**DO YOURSELF A FAVOR**"; love yourself and the life you have received because of Him!
- To keep from sinking, **DON'T LOOK TOO LONG!**
- "**DON'T SEND ME ANY FLOWERS**" after I'm gone. Send some flowers today!
- There will be times we will need to **DRAW THE LINE** and step across it to victory.
- When you feel mentally weighed down, **EMPTY YOUR POCKETS!**
- In all areas of life, concentrate on **FOUR MORE YARDS!**
- When 'back drifting' occurs, **GOING HOME** brings gratefulness and love.
- **HEAR THE HISS-S-S** and keep our gardens safe!
- When we feel, "**I HATE DIETS!**", let's do all to the glory of God.
- When it doesn't appear a change of heart is taking place in our children or others, continue to love and show praise to them. Each of us has a child inside us who feels "**I NEED MY LOVIN'!**"
- If we say, "**I NEVER GOT TO SAY GOODBYE!**", lift our arms to Him.
- When we feel weary, we can say "**I'M DANCING AS HARD AS I CAN!**"
- **IN DUE SEASON** we will reap the fruit of answered prayer.
- When we are struggling to believe for our miracles, the Lord asks us the question "**IS MY ARM TOO SHORT?**"
- We must always **LOAD OUR GUNS!**
- We must exercise our **MENTAL MUSCLES** to God's glory.
- Jesus died to clean out the **MESSY CLOSETS** of our hearts!
- Jesus is saying to us, "**MY CHILD DON'T EVER STOP LOVING ME.**"
- It is **NOT HOW BUT WHO.** Our part is to believe, His part is to answer.
- **OUR RESPONSIBILITY IS TO RECEIVE.**
- When we return home, our **RING AND SANDALS** will be waiting.
- When we see **SYMPTOMS** of sin, recognize its true source and pray!
- Keep **THE SPIRIT OF XMAS** out of our **Christ**mas!
- If **THE WALLS CAME TUMBLING DOWN**, examine the foundation!
- To **WALK IN LOVE** with His children is to give an offering of love to Him.
- We must stay under the covering of His loving, protective **WINGS!**
- When we are tempted to judge others, we should recall the w ords, "**YOU'LL HAVE TO SPEAK UP, SHE'S HARD OF HEARING!**"

Give the gift of
A Favor
to your friends, acquaintances and loved ones.

For additional copies check with your local bookstore or order by sending your check or money order payable to:

NEW VENTURE
P.O. Box 26493 • Greenville, SC 29616 • (864) 292-9095
FAX: (864) 292-9095

I would like ____ copies of "DO YOURSELF A FAVOR" for only $14.95 each, plus $3.00 shipping. (SC residents please add 75¢ state sales tax per book). Canadian orders must have a U.S. funds postal money order.

Shipping:
$3.00 for the first book and $2.00 for each additional book. Allow 3 to 4 weeks for delivery.

My check or money order for $_____ is enclosed.

Print Name: _____

Address: _____

City: _____

State: _____ Zip: _____

Phone: (____) _____

Look forward to the "Favors To Myself Day By Day"calendar, "Favors to Myself Moment by Moment" notepads and audio of the book "DO YOURSELF A FAVOR" to be released in 1999!

145

LET US REMEMBER

- **A LOYAL FRIEND** is a prized possession!
- When you trust in God's faithfulness, you can **BELIEVE FOR YOUR DREAM.**
- No request is too small, not even **CHOCOLATE-COVERED CHERRIES!**
- We should not speak **CORRUPT COMMUNICATIONS** but rather attractive words of grace to the hearers.
- **"DO YOURSELF A FAVOR";** love yourself and the life you have received because of Him!
- To keep from sinking, **DON'T LOOK TOO LONG!**
- **"DON'T SEND ME ANY FLOWERS"** after I'm gone. Send some flowers today!
- There will be times we will need to **DRAW THE LINE** and step across it to victory.
- When you feel mentally weighed down, **EMPTY YOUR POCKETS!**
- In all areas of life, concentrate on **FOUR MORE YARDS!**
- When 'back drifting' occurs, **GOING HOME** brings gratefulness and love.
- **HEAR THE HISS-S-S** and keep our gardens safe!
- When we feel, **"I HATE DIETS!"**, let's do all to the glory of God.
- When it doesn't appear a change of heart is taking place in our children or others, continue to love and show praise to them. Each of us has a child inside us who feels **"I NEED MY LOVIN'!"**
- If we say, **"I NEVER GOT TO SAY GOODBYE!"**, lift our arms to Him.
- When we feel weary, we can say **"I'M DANCING AS HARD AS I CAN!"**
- **IN DUE SEASON** we will reap the fruit of answered prayer.
- When we are struggling to believe for our miracles, the Lord asks us the question **"IS MY ARM TOO SHORT?"**
- We must always **LOAD OUR GUNS!**
- We must exercise our **MENTAL MUSCLES** to God's glory.
- Jesus died to clean out the **MESSY CLOSETS** of our hearts!
- Jesus is saying to us, **"MY CHILD DON'T EVER STOP LOVING ME."**
- It is **NOT HOW BUT WHO.** Our part is to believe, His part is to answer.
- **OUR RESPONSIBILITY IS TO RECEIVE.**
- When we return home, our **RING AND SANDALS** will be waiting.
- When we see **SYMPTOMS** of sin, recognize its true source and pray!
- Keep **THE SPIRIT OF XMAS** out of our **Christ**mas!
- If **THE WALLS CAME TUMBLING DOWN**, examine the foundation!
- To **WALK IN LOVE** with His children is to give an offering of love to Him.
- We must stay under the covering of His loving, protective **WINGS!**
- When we are tempted to judge others, we should recall the words, **"YOU'LL HAVE TO SPEAK UP, SHE'S HARD OF HEARING!"**

Give the gift of
A Favor
to your friends, acquaintances and loved ones.

For additional copies check with your local bookstore or order by sending your check or money order payable to:

NEW VENTURE
P.O. Box 26493 • Greenville, SC 29616 • (864) 292-9095
FAX; (864) 292-9095

I would like ____ copies of "DO YOURSELF A FAVOR" for only $14.95 each, plus $3.00 shipping. (SC residents please add 75¢ state sales tax per book). Canadian orders must have a U.S. funds postal money order.

Shipping :
$3.00 for the first book and $2.00 for each additional book. Allow 3 to 4 weeks for delivery.

My check or money order for $_____ is enclosed.

Print Name: _____

Address: _____

City: _____

State: _____ Zip:_____

Phone: (____) _____

Look forward to the "Favors To Myself Day By Day"calendar, "Favors to Myself Moment by Moment" notepads and audio of the book "DO YOURSELF A FAVOR" to be released in 1999!

LET US REMEMBER

- **A LOYAL FRIEND** is a prized possession!
- When you trust in God's faithfulness, you can **BELIEVE FOR YOUR DREAM.**
- No request is too small, not even **CHOCOLATE-COVERED CHERRIES!**
- We should not speak **CORRUPT COMMUNICATIONS** but rather attractive words of grace to the hearers.
- **"DO YOURSELF A FAVOR";** love yourself and the life you have received because of Him!
- To keep from sinking, **DON'T LOOK TOO LONG!**
- **"DON'T SEND ME ANY FLOWERS"** after I'm gone. Send some flowers today!
- There will be times we will need to **DRAW THE LINE** and step across it to victory.
- When you feel mentally weighed down, **EMPTY YOUR POCKETS!**
- In all areas of life, concentrate on **FOUR MORE YARDS!**
- When 'back drifting' occurs, **GOING HOME** brings gratefulness and love.
- **HEAR THE HISS-S-S** and keep our gardens safe!
- When we feel, **"I HATE DIETS!"**, let's do all to the glory of God.
- When it doesn't appear a change of heart is taking place in our children or others, continue to love and show praise to them. Each of us has a child inside us who feels **"I NEED MY LOVIN'!"**
- If we say, **"I NEVER GOT TO SAY GOODBYE!"**, lift our arms to Him.
- When we feel weary, we can say **"I'M DANCING AS HARD AS I CAN!"**
- **IN DUE SEASON** we will reap the fruit of answered prayer.
- When we are struggling to believe for our miracles, the Lord asks us the question **"IS MY ARM TOO SHORT?"**
- We must always **LOAD OUR GUNS!**
- We must exercise our **MENTAL MUSCLES** to God's glory.
- Jesus died to clean out the **MESSY CLOSETS** of our hearts!
- Jesus is saying to us, **"MY CHILD DON'T EVER STOP LOVING ME."**
- It is **NOT HOW BUT WHO.** Our part is to believe, His part is to answer.
- **OUR RESPONSIBILITY IS TO RECEIVE.**
- When we return home, our **RING AND SANDALS** will be waiting.
- When we see **SYMPTOMS** of sin, recognize its true source and pray!
- Keep **THE SPIRIT OF XMAS** out of our **Christ**mas!
- If **THE WALLS CAME TUMBLING DOWN**, examine the foundation!
- To **WALK IN LOVE** with His children is to give an offering of love to Him.
- We must stay under the covering of His loving, protective **WINGS!**
- When we are tempted to judge others, we should recall the words, **"YOU'LL HAVE TO SPEAK UP, *SHE'S* HARD OF HEARING!"**